CAMBRIDGE
ENGLISH
WORLDWIDE

An A to Z of methodology

ANDREW LITTLEJOHN & DIANA HICKS

CAMBRIDGE
UNIVERSITY PRESS

PUBLISHED BY THE PRESS SYNDICATE OF THE UNIVERSITY OF CAMBRIDGE
The Pitt Building, Trumpington Street, Cambridge, United Kingdom

CAMBRIDGE UNIVERSITY PRESS
The Edinburgh Building, Cambridge CB2 2RU, UK   http://www.cup.cam.ac.uk
40 West 20th Street, New York, NY 10011–4211, USA   http://www.cup.org
10 Stamford Road, Oakleigh, Melbourne 3166, Australia
Ruiz de Alarcón 13, 28014 Madrid, Spain

First published 2000

Printed in the United Kingdom at the University Press, Cambridge

ISBN 0 521 77668 6 An A to Z of methodology

Contents

Introduction

This *A to Z of methodology* is designed to accompany the course *Cambridge English Worldwide* by Andrew Littlejohn and Diana Hicks. *Cambridge English Worldwide* is a course developed especially for young students (around 10–16 years of age). The course features a strong language and grammar element combined with cross-curricular topics which involve students and invite them to share and contribute their own ideas and experiences. For more information about the course, contact your nearest Cambridge University Press representative or visit the following websites:

> http://www.cup.cam.ac.uk/elt
> http://www.cup.cam.ac.uk/elt/ces

You can also find further information at Andrew Littlejohn's home page:

> http://ourworld.compuserve.com/homepages/A_Littlejohn

This *A to Z of methodology* offers background ideas and practical suggestions for English language teaching in general, but with particular reference to *Cambridge English Worldwide*. In the Teacher's Books that accompany the course you will find cross-references to entries in the *A to Z* (for example **AtoZ MOTHER TONGUE**). It is *not* intended that you should read all of the relevant references just to prepare one lesson or that you should read this booklet all at once. It is for *reference*: for you to read at your leisure, as and when you wish. It also contains four articles on different aspects of language teaching.

Some of the entries (see, for example, **GRAMMAR** and **LEARNING STRATEGIES**) also include ideas for how to do some simple 'research' in the classroom. These are practical ideas for finding out more about how your students learn and work, and how you can therefore help them to learn more quickly and effectively.

An A to Z of methodology

Cross-references to other entries in the **AtoZ** are shown in small capitals, **LIKE THIS**.

AtoZ AUTONOMY

What and why?

Autonomy has two main aspects in language teaching. The first concerns the students' *use* of the language. The ultimate goal of most language teaching is to develop the students' autonomy in their own language use. That is, to develop the ability to use the language as they need or want to. This has direct implications for the kind of tasks that students are asked to do. If students are only asked to do 'closed tasks' they are unlikely to develop the ability to use the language with ease. **OPEN-ENDED TASKS** are much more important in this respect.

The second aspect of autonomy, however, concerns how the students *learn*. If all the decisions about learning are always taken by the teacher, the students will not have the opportunity to decide things for themselves. This means that they will not develop the ability to learn by themselves or to work out what works best *for them* as individuals. In a rapidly changing world, however, these abilities are increasingly important as people are continually required to learn new skills and absorb new information. Learning how to learn should thus be a vital component in any educational course.

Practical ideas

- *CEWw* incorporates numerous tasks which require students to **DECIDE** things for themselves, to plan and to

evaluate. You can discuss these tasks with the students so that they understand the value of them in helping them to learn without your direct supervision.
- The Listening and Speaking Pack provides a good support for the students to exercise autonomy in learning. You can spend some time discussing with the students how they use the cassette, when they listen to it, and so on.
- The **HELP YOURSELF** section in the Workbook (Level 1 onwards) offers practical support in developing the students' autonomy in learning. You can read and discuss some of the ideas with the students, and then return to this after a week or so and ask how many of the techniques they have used, why they have or have not done so, and so on.
- The **DECIDE ... EXERCISES** ask students to make decisions. You can increase the number of these in order to encourage the students to take more responsibility. See also **DO IT YOURSELF**.
- After the students have decided something and then carried it out, it is important for them to **EVALUATE** what they have done. You can discuss what they did, how it went and how they could improve it next time.
- Stress to the students that there are a number of vital tools for learning. They need to have a bilingual dictionary, a grammar, notebooks and a cassette player.

AtoZ BRAINSTORMING

What and why?

'Brainstorming' is the name given to a number of techniques used for generating and gathering ideas.
The basic principle is that the students suggest ideas which may be collected, for example, on the blackboard. During the collecting of ideas, *all* ideas suggested are noted down – only after the brainstorming is finished are the ideas discussed, grouped or eliminated. Brainstorming can encourage students to speak out and share ideas. It also gives the teacher an immediate impression of how much the students already know about something.

Practical ideas

There are a number of different ways you can approach brainstorming.

- Write 'What do we know about (name of the topic)?' in big letters on the blackboard. Place a circle round it and some lines out from the circle. Ask the students what they know about the topic. As they say things, write them around the circle.
- Write 'What do we know about (name of the topic)?' in big letters on the blackboard. Give the students a few minutes to note down ideas by themselves. Then collect their ideas on the board.
- As above, but students work in small groups.
- As above, but play some soft **MUSIC** while they are thinking/discussing.
- Students work in groups to generate ideas and then cross-group (see **GROUPWORK**) to compare. You can use different types of **MUSIC** during these stages.

- The brainstorming can be put up on a **POSTER** and referred to and added to over a number of lessons.
- Brainstorming doesn't have to be about things they know. It can be about things they would like to know.

Students can build up a question **POSTER**.
- Brainstorming can be done in English or in the **MOTHER TONGUE**.

A to Z CHECKING ANSWERS

What and why?

After students have done an exercise, it is important that they have an opportunity to check what they have done. This will give them **FEEDBACK** on their work. There are a number of ways in which you can do this.

Practical ideas

- You can go through the answers while the students look at their own work.
- Students can work together and then sit with another pair to check the answers.

- Small groups of students can go through their answers together. During this time, you can circulate around the class, helping and checking.
- You can provide an 'answer sheet' for students to check their own answers. (This can be circulated around the class while students are doing some other activity, pinned up on the board for them to check after the lesson, or written on the blackboard.)
- If students have incorrect answers, you can give hints or clues rather than simply giving the correct answers. This can help them think through the task again and learn more. (See **ERROR CORRECTION**.)

A to Z CRITICAL LANGUAGE AWARENESS

What and why?

In language teaching, we now recognise that language is not simply grammar, but also a system of 'communication'. For this reason, we often involve students in sharing information, using language for special purposes, expressing opinions and so on. One result of a view of language as 'communicating', however, is that it ignores the fact that people do not use language *neutrally*. Language is used not only as a means of sharing ideas, but also as a way of controlling people and influencing what they think and do. Language use involves making choices about lexis, grammar, register, discourse structure, etc., and these choices are often made for particular reasons. For example, a choice of words may be important – an armed group, for instance, might be called 'terrorists' or 'freedom fighters' depending on whose side you are on. Similarly, the passive voice, for example, might be used to hide facts or give authority to a statement as in, for instance, 'Ten million pounds were lost last year.' (We could ask: 'Who lost them? Why? How? "Lost" means what?' and so on.) Register might be used to encourage people to act in certain ways. Advertisements, for example, often use a friendly, familiar tone of voice ('We care for you') to make people feel that a product is important to them personally. Discourse structure can also determine what your 'rights' are in a conversation – as, for example, in a job interview where only one person might have the 'right' to ask questions.

In recent years, this way of looking at language has developed into what is now called 'critical language analysis' and, in schools, many teachers now try to raise the students' awareness of how language is used, so they are not so easily influenced by others. The word 'critical', here, does not mean 'negative' but 'careful, thoughtful'. (See also **CRITICAL PEDAGOGY**.)

Practical ideas

- If you start from the assumption that language use involves making choices, you can ask students 'Why did they say *that*?', 'Why did they use *that* word rather than another word?', 'Why did they use that tense?', 'What are they *not* saying?' and so on.
- There are many words in English that are typically only used when talking about women, or about men or about children, and this may affect the way we think about people. For example, 'gossip' is typically associated with women, while men might 'talk'. You can give the students a list of words and ask them to categorise them and then discuss *why* they have categorised them that way. For example, they could try to categorise the following words into 'About women', 'About men', 'About boys', 'About girls': beautiful, strong, trustworthy, silly, pretty, mature, gossip, weak, handsome, rough, ambitious. If they put some words in two or more categories, you can discuss how the word changes its meaning.
- You can encourage students to think about statements about things and ask if they are 'negative', 'positive' or 'neutral'.
- If the students read a news story, you can ask how the story would change if someone else was reporting it. For example, if the story is about a strike in a factory, how would the story change if the strikers reported it, or the employers, or the government, or customers?
- You can encourage students to think about what the writer thinks about the reader. For example, if you look at an advertisement, what type of people is it appealing to? Does the advertisement suggest (even implicitly) that certain things are desirable? How does the advertisement do this?

- If there are words in English in public places in your country or if English is creeping into the students' mother tongue, you could ask students to consider why, in each case, English is used. Some writers talk about 'linguistic imperialism' to describe how English is entering into other languages.
- You can ask students to think about mother tongue language use too: which words are used mainly by young people? Which words are more 'official'? Can they think of any English equivalents?
- You can ask the students to look at the conversations in the *Out and about* sections and to choose one of the characters. If that character changed to, for example, 'head teacher' how would the language change?

AtoZ CRITICAL PEDAGOGY

What and why?

Language teaching is increasingly being seen as a part of education, and as such has a responsibility towards the students' whole personality and educational and social development. Some teachers have taken this idea further and argue that teaching should try to develop the students' ability to QUESTION, to think for themselves and ultimately take more control over their lives. To do this, these teachers choose topics which will provoke discussion and thought, and encourage students to criticise. They also try to bring about more STUDENT INVOLVEMENT and try to develop the students' sense of AUTONOMY. Many of these ideas have been built into *CEWw*. A number of topics require students to think about wider social issues – the environment, the effects of television, ethnic minorities and so on. The methodology of *CEWw* also aims to develop the students' ability to think for themselves and organise their own learning through such things as the HELP YOURSELF section in the Workbook, the DECIDE … EXERCISES and the EVALUATION sections.

Practical ideas

- Many of the topics in *CEWw* can be used as a starting-point for students to think about and investigate their own society. Students can work in small groups on a project and report back to the class, or you can allow time for DISPLAYING STUDENTS' WORK.
- If you think that most of the students are likely to have the same opinion about something, you can ask some of them to prepare an argument against it. You can then involve them in class DISCUSSIONS or get them to prepare POSTERS with their ideas.
- You can involve the students in planning some part of the work they will do in class over the next few weeks. For this you can require that they make decisions and plan what they will do. See DO IT YOURSELF for more ideas.
- Critical pedagogy also encourages students to be aware or critical of their *own* attitudes, values and prejudices. A text or situation may provoke reactions in the students which you can encourage them to question and discuss.

AtoZ CURRICULUM LINKS

What and why?

One of the main features of *CEWw* is that it makes direct links between English language learning and the school curriculum. This happens in two ways. Firstly, there are links with broader educational aims, such as developing PROBLEM-SOLVING abilities, AUTONOMY, QUESTIONING, cooperative learning and so on. Secondly, there are direct links with school subjects, such as Science, Geography, History and so on. There are a number of reasons why this is important. Language teaching *is* a part of education, and needs to take its full educational responsibility. A cross-curricular approach also offers students an ideal opportunity to refresh and revise what they have done in other subject areas and to make links with what they have learnt so that their knowledge becomes more active. This makes both learning *and* teaching English more interesting and more memorable. Working with subject knowledge that is important and interesting in its own right makes it more likely that students will remember the language associated with it. Finally, whether language teaching has explicit links with the curriculum or not, it is clear that it can have a role in shaping the broader attitudes and abilities of students. It thus makes sense to take this fact into account and build it into our language teaching methodology.

Practical ideas

- Teaching English through a cross-curricular approach can mean that your role as a teacher changes. Many teachers report that cross-curricular teaching is more interesting, since it involves *their* learning as well. However, you are an *English* teacher and you cannot be expected to know all about Science, Geography and so on. Your role as a teacher, then, is to stimulate the students to find the information/answers/ explanations that they require for themselves.
- In the notes to the Unit in the Teacher's Book, you will find some background information on some of the topics covered in *CEWw*.
- You may find it useful to talk to teachers of other subject areas. As you approach a new Theme, you could find out what work the students will do or have done in that area.

- It may be possible to teach some lessons together with another subject teacher. For example, with some advance preparation, students could do Science experiments, Maths, Physical Education and so on in English. You could choose a new topic area together.

- As you begin a new Theme, you could start with a question **POSTER**. You can ask the students questions such as: 'What questions from History connect to this?', 'How does Geography connect to this?', 'Is Maths important for this topic?', 'How?' and so on.

AtoZ DECIDE ... EXERCISES

What and why?

Decide ... exercises come in a number of places in the Student's Book, particularly in the *Topic* and *Language* Units, the *Out and about* sections, and the *Culture matters* sections. They give the students a choice of what they can do next. One option is usually to decide for themselves what they want to do (see **DO IT YOURSELF**). The students can do the *Decide ...* exercises alone, in pairs or in small groups. The exercises are designed as a first step in the students taking responsibility for their own learning (see **STUDENT INVOLVEMENT**).

Practical ideas

- Explain the choices clearly to the class before they start. Allow enough time for them to decide which task to do and how to work (alone/in pairs, etc.).
- Make sure there is enough time left in the lesson to make a start.
- While the class is working, go round and offer help if needed (see **MONITORING AND GUIDING**).
- Students can also use the *Help yourself list* (or *Ideas list*) at the back of the Student's Book for ideas of things they can do.
- If students finish early, they can work on the **TIME TO SPARE?** tasks, fill in their **LANGUAGE RECORD** or choose from/contribute to the **EXERCISE BOX**.

AtoZ DISCIPLINE

What and why?

One difficulty frequently encountered by teachers of secondary-age students is the problem of maintaining discipline. There are two main aspects to consider in this. The first is to ask 'What kind of discipline do I want?'. The key should be to maintain a purposeful but relaxed atmosphere in the classroom, where certain students don't disturb other students. This may mean that some so-called discipline problems are not real problems at all. As long as the overall atmosphere is conducive to learning, it may not be worth making an issue out of minor acts of 'misbehaviour'. If students were 100% compliant, we would have reason to be worried! On the other hand, discipline can, at times, become a serious problem. The important question to consider here is *'Why* are they behaving like that?'. The cause of discipline problems may lie in difficulties at home, in school or with friends. These are likely to be beyond your control. Some causes of discipline problems, however, may lie within your classroom and you may be able to resolve them.

Practical ideas

- If the problem recurs, try to discuss it with the students. Approach the issue as *their* problem as well as yours ('We've got a problem. Our lesson/groupwork, etc. is not working, is it? What can we do about it?'). This can give them a feeling of responsibility. For this, you will need to listen to their views and be ready to make changes.

- If you have a large class, and particularly if it contains students with **MIXED ABILITIES**, discipline problems may be caused by students who feel left out or who don't understand what is happening. This may be because the work that has been set is not suitable for their level of ability. Using **GROUPWORK** and providing different levels of support can help them feel more involved.
- Discipline problems may occur during listening activities. This may be because some students cannot hear the cassette very well. They may be 'lost' before the lesson really starts. Tell them to look at the words in the book while they listen if the room is noisy.
- If the students are restless or tired, you could start with some **PHYSICAL MOVEMENT**.
- The **PACE** and **TIMING** of the lessons may be too fast for some of the students and so they get lost, feel they can never catch up, and then begin to misbehave. These slower students may prefer to work individually.
- Make sure that the work of the weaker students has equal feedback.
- Try to bring about more **STUDENT INVOLVEMENT**, especially from those students who are causing disruption.
- To settle students down when they come into the class, you can use **MUSIC** or regular journal writing. A journal is a book that the students write in which you do not correct or look at unless invited to do so. The students may write anything they like about their day, their feelings, the things they have done, the things they have learnt and so on. Initially, this will be in the **MOTHER TONGUE** but you can encourage them to try to write in English as the course goes on.

- During group or pairwork, give extra help to troublesome students.
- Changing the seating arrangements can help to reduce discipline problems. If there is a large empty space between you and the students, this can make it difficult to create a sense of being 'a class'. If you move closer to the students, and (where possible) sit with them in a circle, this can help to focus their attention on the lesson.
- Get the troublesome students to work on something you know they are good at and which will give them a feeling of achievement. You can give them some other individual responsibility for a term. For example, being in charge of the **EXERCISE BOX**, collecting in **HOMEWORK**, helping with the **DISPLAYS**, leading the singing in **SONGS**.
- Try not to give extra English homework as a punishment; it can create the view that English is boring or difficult, or both!
- See also **TEACHING ADOLESCENTS**.
- If discipline becomes a serious problem, the most important point is to avoid getting into confrontation with the students. This only makes matters worse. Dealing effectively with serious discipline problems requires getting the students willingly on your side. Try to remain calm, but firm.

A*to*Z DISCUSSIONS

What and why?

Discussions can allow students the opportunity to give their own ideas and, in the later stages of the course, to practise using English to say what they want to say. They can also form a way into a topic which can stimulate the students' imagination and give the teacher an indication of how much the students already know. It is important, however – particularly when discussions are in English – that the emphasis is always on the *ideas* which are being expressed, not on the accuracy of the grammar and pronunciation. A heavy emphasis on form can block a discussion and prevent ideas from emerging.

Practical ideas

- Discussions can be approached through **BRAINSTORMING**.
- If the topic is fairly complex or technical, then you can have a brief discussion in the mother tongue. In the upper levels of *CEWw*, you should be able to use English most of the time in class, but a brief **MOTHER TONGUE** discussion can give the students the feeling that their ideas and contributions are valued.
- As the students' abilities in English develop, you can encourage them to express their ideas in English. If the students show resistance, you might ask them 'Would you like to know how to say that in English?' and show them how they can express the same idea in English.
- Discussions in the mother tongue can be used as a way to introduce the vocabulary that they will meet in English. After a brief discussion, you can put words on the board and ask if they know how to say those things in English.
- Students of this age are often concerned with what is 'right' and sometimes have very strong, apparently fixed ideas about things. You can ask students to prepare an argument in favour of or against something so that they are forced to think about the other side of an argument. Class discussion can then take the form of a debate between opposing sides. This is particularly useful if you are interested in developing a **CRITICAL PEDAGOGY**.
- Discussions are probably best kept short (maximum 10 minutes). Beyond that, students may lose interest or the discussion may lose its focus.
- With a clear, concrete focus, students can work briefly in small groups. Some groups can then offer feedback to the whole class.

A*to*Z DISPLAYING STUDENTS' WORK

What and why?

At the end of many tasks in *CEWw*, particularly the optional *Activity* Units and work for the **PARCEL OF ENGLISH**, students will have produced a large piece of work. To give them a sense of purpose about their work, it is a good idea to display it.

Practical ideas

- Pin work up on the classroom wall for a week or so and then change it. Perhaps you can display work in the corridors, in the school hall, in the school foyer, in the canteen, in the staffroom or in other subject rooms (for cross-curricular links). (You can also ask students for display ideas.)
- Take a photograph of the display for reference.
- Make sure you write on the display the students' names, their class, the subject of the work and a description of the purpose of the work (in the **MOTHER TONGUE**, if necessary).
- When you take the work down, the students can either keep their work in their own 'Activity file' or put it in a large scrapbook.
- Encourage students to help you display work.
- Display pictures as well as the writing – some students may be better at Art than English!

- Some students may be sensitive about showing their work to others – it may be best to ask them if they want to.

- If a display is put up in the classroom or put out on the class tables, allow time for the students to walk around to read it. One member from each group can stand by their work to explain and talk about what they have done (see also **POSTERS**).

A to Z DO IT YOURSELF

What and why?

'Do it yourself' is an important idea that occurs throughout *CEWw*. Encouraging students to do something *themselves*, rather than simply using the exercises in the book, is to encourage them towards **AUTONOMY** – the ultimate goal of education. This also allows students room for their own individual interests, needs and abilities. It is also an important element in a **CRITICAL PEDAGOGY**. 'Do it yourself' occurs as a feature of the **DECIDE ... EXERCISES**, and is supported through the **HELP YOURSELF LIST** (or *Ideas list*) in the Student's Book. In the *Decide ...* exercises, the students must decide what they wish to do, in consultation with you. Initially, it is likely that the suggestions that students make for what they would like to do are not ones that you think are particularly valuable. This may not be a problem for a number of reasons. Firstly, one of the aims of allowing students to suggest something else to do is to bring about greater **STUDENT INVOLVEMENT** and a feeling of 'ownership' of what they are learning. Secondly, it is *only* through making decisions that students can become better at making decisions. The important point is that any suggestion they make and act on should be followed up by some kind of **EVALUATION**. This can be simply asking the students how useful they found what they did.

Practical ideas

- If students cannot think of something to do, you can *propose* something. In the Student's Book there is a list of suggestions with each *Decide ...* exercise. There are also other possibilities, if the students wish to do something completely different, for example: choose something from the **EXERCISE BOX** if you have one in class, do some **READING**, look back through the previous Unit, do something from the Workbook, do a **TIME TO SPARE?** exercise, prepare something for the **PARCEL OF ENGLISH**, or design an exercise using the **HELP YOURSELF** section in the Workbook.
- One or two lessons before the students come to a *Decide ...* exercise, point out the option for them to decide for themselves. Encourage them to prepare ahead.
- You will need to insist that what they decide to do is related to learning English!
- You could also allow some time for students to tell other students (either in small groups or to the whole class) what they have been doing.

A to Z ERRORS AND ERROR CORRECTION

What and why?

Making errors is an inevitable and necessary part of language learning. It is only through making errors, and hearing the correct forms, that students can develop their own understanding of how English works. It is thus important that students have as much opportunity as possible to produce language and, with the focus on using English creatively (rather than simply repeating language), the number of errors that students make will inevitably rise. Teachers thus need to think carefully about how they will respond to these errors.

The process of absorbing a new language structure takes considerable time. Teachers cannot, therefore, expect that simply correcting an error will produce immediate results. Some errors can remain even up to very advanced levels (such as the 's' in 'she lives', 'he goes', etc.). A strong emphasis on error correction cannot be expected to produce students who make few errors. In fact, an over-emphasis on error correction is likely to be counter-productive as students become deterred from using – and experimenting

with – new language and vocabulary. But students *do* need to have their errors pointed out to them. The key is to limit correction to a small number of points at a time and to judge when the right moment for correction is.

Practical ideas

- The **HELP YOURSELF** section in the Workbook includes ideas on students' checking of their own work.
- Correcting students when they are in the middle of saying something may produce students who are afraid to talk. You can make a note of the errors students make and go through them at the end of the discussion/lesson.
- Limit yourself to correcting only a few errors in written work or after the students speak.
- For errors in **WRITING**, students can be encouraged to build up a short list of their most common errors. The list can be arranged to form a mnemonic of things to check (e.g. PATTIBS = plurals, articles, tenses, 'there is/are', '-ing' form, 'be', spelling).

In monolingual classes most students will make the same errors. You may want to have 'an error of the week' game. Choose an error which most students make, tell them what it is and write the correct version on a piece of paper on the wall. This raises the students' consciousness about this particular error. They then have to try not to make this error all week. The student who succeeds can choose the 'error of the week' for the next week.

AtoZ EVALUATION

What and why?

There are two main ways in which evaluation is important in learning. The first way is in relation to *what* and *how much* students have learned – such as through tests and quizzes (see **TESTS**). The second way, however, is in relation to *how* or *in what way* the students are learning, as a group and as individual learners. The first aspect of evaluation is the most common in language teaching, although the second aspect is of equal importance to learning and understanding. The aim of this second kind of evaluation is to encourage the students to look at the different ways they can learn and identify the 'best' ones for them. This means that they can gradually take more control over the way they learn and, at the same time, you, the teacher, can get a clearer insight into how the students approach language learning.

In *CEWw*, evaluation is introduced in various places. At the lower levels, there are evaluation questions after the students have done an optional *Activity* Unit. These questions ask them, for example, how well they have worked in groups, whether they liked writing poems and so on. From *CEWw 3* onwards, regular *Evaluation* sections ask the students to think about *how* they approach different aspects of learning English, such as preparing for tests, doing homework, remembering new language and so on.

Practical ideas

- For practical ideas in the *what* and *how much* aspects of evaluation, see **TESTS**.
- Avoid, initially at least, asking the students questions such as 'What things did you like?' 'What things didn't you like?' Negative questions tend to produce negative answers. It is better to ask 'What do you think about …?'
- You can ask the students to give you feedback in writing (in the mother tongue), anonymously. You can ask them, for example, to list exercises in order of difficulty (e.g. mark exercises on a line from 'easy to difficult'), to say where they think they need / would like more practice, to say how fast/slowly they think things are going, what problems they think they have with English or what things they would like explained again.
- Evaluation by the students requires the teacher to be open to listen and discuss, and make changes if necessary.
- Initially, it is likely that the students' evaluation of how they have been learning will be very superficial. Just like learning itself, evaluation requires practice. The more they do it, the better they will become at it, and the more able they will become to accept responsibility.

- You could place a Suggestion Box in the classroom in the second or third week of your course and encourage students to put in it their evaluations of different tasks and texts as they work through a Unit. This could provide the basis for discussion at the end of the Theme.

Researching the classroom

- Before giving the students a **TEST**, give them a list of what they will be tested on. Then, before they do the test, ask them to write down what mark they think they will get in each part. If you do this before each test, you can see if the students' ability to assess their own strengths in English improves, and if the gap between what they *think* they will get and what they *actually* get, closes.
- After a lesson, ask the students to write down a list of what they think they learnt in that lesson. Think back over the lesson (or tape-record it) and try to identify *when* and *how* the things that they remembered came up. Do this for a few lessons to see if a pattern emerges.
- If you have one or more classes using this coursebook, you can involve one class in a lot more evaluation discussions. You can then see if more student evaluation activities produce more involved learners. You could give each class an anonymous questionnaire to discover how much time they devote to English in a week, how high their motivation is, which aspects they like best and so on. In the long term, you could also see if more student evaluation/planning activities produce better abilities in English.
- You could ask some students to keep a diary of their studies in English, of what precisely they study outside the classroom, of how long they spend on it and so on. This could also give you some idea of the **LEARNING STRATEGIES** they use.
- You could interview a few students to find out how they go about their studies. A word association technique is very useful in giving a 'snapshot' of the students' impressions. Read out a list of key areas in language learning, and after each one pause for a minute or so. Ask the students to note down their thoughts in relation to that area. This can be anonymous, of course. You can then collect the papers to get a picture of what is going on in the students' heads. Key areas might be: topic lessons, grammar, listening to English in class, writing in English, and so on. You could also try word association on how they feel about things to do with English, English culture and so on (which will be related to their motivation). Key areas might be: English, 'Me speaking English', English things, English-speaking people, 'my English book', 'doing English homework', and so on.

AtoZ EXERCISE BOX

What and why?

An Exercise Box is a box that you can have in class in which you put exercises that the students design for each other. (This idea is introduced in Levels 1 and 2 of *CEWw*.) Each class can have its own Exercise Box which can be a small cardboard box or shoe box with cardboard dividers. This, ideally, should be kept in the classroom or taken to every lesson. The purpose of an Exercise Box is to bring about more **STUDENT INVOLVEMENT** in their language course. Students can learn a great deal by designing exercises.

Practical ideas

- You can ask students to design exercises for each other after you have read through a text (see **INSIDE THE TEXT**) or when you have completed a Unit or Theme. Alternatively, some students can design some exercises if they have **TIME TO SPARE**.
- The **HELP YOURSELF LIST** (or *Ideas list*) at the back of the Student's Book gives many ideas for different tasks that students can design.
- Instead of asking students to do an exercise for homework, you can ask them to make one.
- You can check through a student-designed exercise to ensure that it is correct. Students can write a neat, correct version of their exercise on a blank postcard which they can put into the box. They should put the answers on the back.
- Students can take an exercise from the box if they finish a task before the others or if they find the other class work too difficult.
- The Exercise Box will gradually build up to offer a source of revision and/or remedial work.
- For easy reference, label the exercises, showing what Unit they come from. You can divide the box into sections for each Unit. You may want to colour-code the exercises for difficulty.
- You can add your own exercises to the box, of course.
- Student-designed **TESTS** can also be put in the Exercise Box.

AtoZ FEEDBACK

What and why?

In learning, one of the most important factors is a feeling that you are getting somewhere. For some students, learning at school can seem like an endless list of exercises, in which they move from one task to the next. This can lead to a lack of a sense of direction in their learning or a feeling that there is no value in it. It is important, therefore, that students receive feedback on what they have done and that their effort is recognised and valued. Feedback may focus on the *form* of what they have done (spelling, grammar, neatness, etc.) or on its *content* (its message, the opinions and ideas expressed). As teachers, we typically respond to the form aspect, but it is only through the content aspect that we can really recognise our students as individuals with their own ideas. Feedback is also extremely important in helping students to progress.

Research shows that students monitor who gets positive feedback and who doesn't. They quickly work out who the teacher thinks are 'good' students and who are 'bad' students. This can have an impact on their self-image as learners, so that they can begin to form attitudes such as 'I didn't do well in the test because I'm not very clever' or 'I never do well, so what's the point of trying?'

Practical ideas

- Feedback can come from other students as well as from the teacher. Allowing time for students to show their work to each other (if they wish – this may be a sensitive point) can allow them an opportunity to have pride in their work, ask questions about things they are unsure of, and share ideas.
- If the students are engaged in a large activity, allow some time at the end for them to **DISPLAY THEIR WORK**.
- Feedback between students is best done in pairs or threes with students who are friends with each other.
- Feedback between students can be given a clear focus by asking them to produce a *single* rewritten version of their work which draws on what each of them has done. For example, if they have completed a guided piece of writing, they can produce a new version which has corrected spellings and grammar, extra ideas, etc.
- In feedback to each other, students may be over-critical or focus only on the form aspect. One way to overcome this is to insist that they make positive suggestions for improvement. Comments may also be limited to two or three points.
- Feedback to you, as the teacher, can be gained through the **EVALUATION** activities.
- In giving students feedback, it is very important that we praise *all* students for the efforts they have made. If students feel that their work has been noticed and is appreciated, they are more likely to work harder.
- Make a conscious effort to praise not only the 'good' students. Try to give positive feedback to all students. This doesn't mean that you have to accept poor work. It means that in your feedback you show students how they can improve. For example, you might say 'This is a

good try. I liked reading about ... There are still quite a few spelling mistakes, though. When you have finished writing, you could check some of the words with a dictionary or the *Wordlist* in your book. Do you want to try next time?'

AtoZ FLUENCY

What and why?

Many language learning tasks focus on accuracy. These are often 'closed' exercises in which there is only one correct answer. Fluency tasks, on the other hand, are more open. They encourage the learners to take risks and be more creative with the language because there is no 'right' or 'wrong' answer (see **OPEN-ENDED TASKS**; also the **HELP YOURSELF LIST** or *Ideas list* in the Student's Book for examples of closed and open tasks). At lower language levels, language teaching has traditionally emphasised accuracy, believing that fluency comes once the grammar has been mastered. In *CEWw*, however, both accuracy and fluency are emphasised right from the beginning. Developing fluency is important in building up the students' confidence and maintaining a sense of achievement in being able to say something meaningful. Many students also learn more naturally through tasks which focus on *using* the language, rather than learning *about* the language. Accuracy, however, is important and for this reason both aspects appear in the tasks in the Student's Book and Workbook.

In all four skills, confidence and fluency are linked and make the students more receptive to learning. Confidence and fluency in **READING** and **LISTENING** help students to deal with language without feeling the need to understand every word, encourage them to guess new words, and enable them to understand the main message, including the speaker's/writer's attitude. Confidence and fluency in **WRITING** and **SPEAKING** allow students to get their ideas across without being restricted by an over-concern with form.

Practical ideas

- There are numerous fluency activities throughout *CEWw*. In the *Topic* and *Language* Units, in particular, you can see how the tasks move from a focus on fluency to a focus on accuracy and then back to fluency.
- In fluency exercises, the focus is on developing and expressing ideas. There is nothing wrong with

correcting language **ERRORS** as they arise, but don't let this obscure the main focus. Make a note of significant language errors and return to them later.
- There is only one way to become fluent and accurate at the same time: through using the language to express/understand ideas. This takes time, so you will need to expect and tolerate language errors as students develop this ability.
- In fluency-focused exercises, try to react to what the students say, not how they say it. For example, if you are marking their written work, you can add a response to what they have said, your opinion on the topic and so on.

Researching the classroom

- Where possible, keep a record of what the students have produced in a fluency exercise (e.g. written work or a recording of a **ROLE PLAY** or **DISCUSSION**). Compare it with what they produce some weeks or months later to get an idea of their development.
- Language errors or a lack of fluency may be caused by the situation in which the students are working. Record some class discussions and some small group work and compare what happened. Are students more fluent and/or accurate when they are talking about particular topics? Is the size of the group important? Is small group work more effective for developing fluency?
- Make a note of the errors that you correct and notice when and how those errors come up again. Many teachers say that students make the same mistakes time and time again because the students don't think before they speak/write. In truth, they are thinking about something else. What is it? Is the message more important to the students?
- Experiment with providing different levels of control and support over what the students speak/write. Do students produce more or less when a topic is left very open and language is not controlled? Try out different **OPEN-ENDED** and closed exercises and compare the results.

AtoZ FOUR SKILLS

What and why?, Practical ideas

See **LISTENING**, **SPEAKING**, **READING** and **WRITING**.

Researching the classroom

- Many teachers assume that the most effective way to learn is orally (through listening and speaking). Writing and reading are seen as practice stages in learning. If you have several classes, you could involve one class in

considerably more in-class writing and reading. You could then see if there appears to be a direct effect on their abilities in English. See **WRITING**, **INTERACTIVE WRITING** and **READING**.
- You could vary your approach to each of the skills and see if that affects what the students produce. For example, you could sometimes ask students to first write 'fluently', without stopping to check, before they

go back to read and revise what they have done. At other times, you could ask them to plan what they will write and to think carefully about each sentence as they write. You could try similar experiments with the other skills. For reading, ask the students to sometimes read quickly through a text without checking words, and at other times to read carefully. For listening, you could play a text straight through for a general impression before going back for details. At other times, you could play it in small sections. For speaking, you could sometimes ask the students to do a **ROLE PLAY** without preparation, and at other times you could ask them to prepare in writing first. Different students will work best in different ways. By experimenting, you can see how individual students respond to each approach.

- If the focus is on one main skill, you can see whether involving the other skills first produces a better result. For example, if you want the students to write something, you could see if their production is improved if they first read and speak about, and then listen to a text about the topic.
- Identify what you think is the students' weakest skill. You could experiment to see if it is possible to improve that skill by directly involving their stronger skills. For example, if the students seem weakest at reading, you could involve them in writing or speaking about a topic before they read about it. If writing is their weakest skill, you could ask them to read and speak about a topic first and to note down useful phrases or ideas for their own writing.

AtoZ GRAMMAR

What and why?

An understanding of the grammar of English is crucial to the development of the students' language learning. By the time students reach secondary school age, they are able to handle and understand grammatical rules and descriptions. With the limited amount of time which the classroom provides for language learning, grammar can be a vital tool in speeding up the students' ability to produce 'correct', meaningful English. In order to see how the language 'jigsaw' fits together, it is also important that students learn to use words such as 'noun', 'verb', 'adjective', etc. This will enable them to work things out for themselves (see **INDUCTIVE GRAMMAR**) and you, the teacher, to explain things to them.

Practical ideas

- The *Language Record* pages ask students to make notes about the grammar they have learned. The *Language Records* thus help to develop a self-created reference for revision.
- Students can write their own **TESTS** as a creative practice to check their own understanding.
- To make sure that students understand the metalanguage, they can write the main words – 'noun', 'verb', 'adjective', 'personal pronoun', etc. – on a **POSTER** on the wall with examples underneath, to act as a reminder.
- As they discover the main grammatical rules and structures, students can construct a poster for the wall with example sentences underneath each main rule.
- The main rules can be written on a sheet by some of the students and placed, for reference, in a class **EXERCISE BOX**.
- Grammar games are often a useful way of practising language. These can be combined with **PHYSICAL MOVEMENT**. For example, to practise the comparative forms, you can ask one of the students to come towards

you saying 'Peter, please come here because you are smaller/bigger/prettier/younger/older (etc.) than I am.' One of the other students then invites you to walk to them and gives a reason using the comparative form. That student is then invited by another student, and so on. Similar games can be played which ask students to perform particular actions when they hear a noun, a verb or an adjective.

Researching the classroom

- How effective is explicit teaching of grammar? Some writers argue that grammar teaching has very little impact on the language that students produce spontaneously. Look carefully at the work that your students have written or record part of a lesson or some small group work. Can you trace the language structures that the students use *directly* to things that they have been taught? Are there some grammatical forms that they are using that they have not been taught?
- Choose an area of grammar from one of the *Language focus* Units, for example some Past simple irregular verbs or the use of 'enough'. Don't teach that area explicitly or ask the students to do any language focus exercises on that area, but otherwise carry on teaching as usual. After a couple of weeks, give the students a short test and include items on the area you chose to see if the students learned it 'naturally' anyway.
- Some areas of grammar seem to be acquired much later than other areas. Talk to teachers of students who have a higher level of English language ability or think about other classes you have. What 'typical errors' do higher level students make? Are they different from the 'typical errors' of lower level students? What areas are in common? When are those areas taught to the students? Can you experiment with changing the order in which language areas are taught?

AtoZ GRAMMAR RECORD

See **LANGUAGE RECORD**.

AtoZ GROUPWORK

What and why?

Groupwork in *CEWw* is based on the idea that students can learn language and information from each other. The principle of cooperative learning is basic to classroom education. It also allows the opportunity for teachers to help with individual problems, for stronger and weaker students to work at their own **PACE** (see **MONITORING AND GUIDING**) and for more students to get more practice.

Practical ideas

- Before students begin groupwork, make sure they know exactly what they are expected to do. Make the focus clear with a definite outcome (for example, to write something or to make a list of something).
- During the lesson note which students are working together so that you can encourage them to work with different people next time.
- After working in groups, students can be cross-grouped. This involves groups re-forming with representatives of the other groups (for example, if students are labelled A, B, C and D in their groups, cross-groups can be formed by all the As coming together, all the Bs, all the Cs and so on). In their cross-groups, students can compare ideas.
- Three or four are probably the best numbers for groupwork.
- There are many ways to set up groups. Try to vary the basis on which you group students: (1) students can choose who to work with; (2) they can turn round and work with the students behind / in front of / next to them; (3) they can be grouped according to ability; (4) they can be grouped alphabetically, according to birth months; (5) they can be grouped to maintain a balance of boys and girls; (6) they can be grouped by numbering students 1, 2, 3, 4 around the class; (7) you can cut up some postcards and distribute the pieces round the class – students have to find who has the pieces which go

with theirs and thus form a group; (8) you can give out cards with names of animals (four of each) – students have to walk around the class making the noise of the animal to find out who is in their group.

Researching the classroom

- Vary the way in which you set up groups (see above). Monitor how the students work when they are grouped differently.
- If groupwork is not functioning well, ask the students to draw up their own 'Rules for Groupwork' which they will agree to follow.
- Monitor the type of **TASKS** which you give students in groups. Which kind of tasks produce most interaction? Do closed or **OPEN-ENDED** tasks produce more discussion?
- Keep a record of how the students appeared to work in their groups – well, cooperatively, noisily, unfocused, and so on. Also keep a record of the details of the groupwork: who was working with whom, what they were doing in groups, what time of day it was, when they did it in the lesson, what preceded the groupwork and so on. After a few lessons, you may be able to see a pattern in what affects the groupwork.
- Studies have shown that the way students are labelled can affect how they perform. For example, students labelled 'good students' tend to work hard, while students who are labelled 'weak' tend to find their work difficult. (This is known as 'the self-fulfilling prophecy'.) You can give each group a name which flatters them, to see if this affects the way they work. For example, 'Brilliant Students: red group', 'Brilliant Students: green group', and so on.
- If you put students into ability groups, tell the weakest students that they will find the work you give them very easy. You can see if this increases their confidence in their work.

AtoZ HELP YOURSELF LIST

What and why?

The *Help yourself list* is a list of types of exercises at the back of the Student's Book at most levels of *CEWw*. It is called *Ideas list* in Student's Book 1. The list is intended to help the students design their own practice exercises for themselves, for the **EXERCISE BOX** or when they are doing **DECIDE … EXERCISES**. Designing exercises increases the amount of **STUDENT INVOLVEMENT** with the course and their own learning, supports a general movement towards **AUTONOMY** and promotes deeper levels of understanding. From *CEWw 3* onwards, the *Help yourself list* is divided into two sections: closed exercises, which only have one correct answer, and open-ended exercises, which do not have a single correct answer.

Practical ideas

- Students can also use the *Help yourself list* (or *Ideas list*) if they have **TIME TO SPARE**.
- You can encourage the students to bring in their own examples of English. They can then use the *Help yourself list* (or *Ideas list*) to make some exercises for themselves and other students.

- Students may be able to add more examples to the list. (These can perhaps be put on the wall.) For example, students may be able to think of ideas to use with pictures, objects, listening passages or writing.
- If stronger students are placed with weaker students, they can help the weaker ones.

AtoZ HELP YOURSELF

What and why?

The idea of helping students to help themselves occurs in a number of places in *CEWw*. From Level 1 onwards, the Workbooks include optional Units which show the students how they can improve their spelling, how they can use a dictionary, how they can get extra grammar practice and so on. From Level 3 onwards, the Student's Books include *Evaluation* sections which ask them to think about their approach to such things as tests, groupwork, doing their homework and so on. The main purpose in these sections is to support the students in developing their **AUTONOMY** and to bring about greater **STUDENT INVOLVEMENT**.

Practical ideas

- To discover how the students use their dictionaries, what they think about spelling, what difficulties their think they have, and so on, you could ask them to make a questionnaire for other students. This will tell you a lot about what they think is important and also show you where they need extra support.

- After the students have discussed their answers to an *Evaluation* questionnaire (Student's Book from *CEWw 3* onwards), you could ask them to make posters of *DOs* and *DON'Ts* in that area; for example, *DOs* and *DON'Ts* about groupwork, about preparing for tests, etc.
- You could choose an area to focus on for one or two weeks and after each lesson ask the students what that they have done. For example, you could ask them what use they have made of a dictionary, what they have done with any new words they have learnt, how they have prepared themselves for a test. You may find that they have nothing much to say – in which case you will have signalled to them that it is something they need to think about!
- Before asking students to do a task, spend a few minutes discussing *how* they will do the task. For example, what they will do when they come to a word they don't understand, or how they will plan their groupwork.

AtoZ HOMEWORK

What and why?

In *CEWw*, homework gives students time to absorb, process and practise what they have learned at school. It also keeps the students involved between lessons and maintains their commitment to learning English. In most courses, the amount of time available in class is simply not sufficient for language learning to take place fast enough. Extra work outside class is essential.

Practical ideas

- *CEWw 3* Student's Book includes a questionnaire for students about how they approach homework.
- Before you set homework, make sure that the students know which exercises they have to do and how long they are expected to spend on their homework. (No more than half an hour is recommended.)
- There are no answers in the Workbook so their homework will have to be checked in the next lesson. You will need to allow some time for this and to build it in as part of the lesson.

- There are a number of ways in which you can correct homework (see *Notes on the Workbook* in the Teacher's Book).
- If you set homework but find that students do not do it, you need to consider why this is happening. There may be a number of possible reasons. It may be too difficult or too easy. They may not have time because of other commitments. They may not see the point of it. They may not have the book! They may have other personal problems. You may be able to resolve these problems by talking to the students, agreeing with them when they can do their homework, discussing whether they find it too easy/difficult, and so on. Perhaps they can sometimes suggest something to do for homework. (Everybody doesn't always have to do the same thing.)

Researching the classroom

- Talk to the students about homework, what they think about it and why it is necessary. Ask them what kinds of homework they find most enjoyable. Ask for ideas of what they would like to do for homework.

- You could also find out what the students think by giving them a questionnaire, or by interviewing a few students.
- Experiment with different kinds of homework to see if it affects the students' response: homework that requires research, homework that requires them to find/make things; homework exercises; homework they can record on cassette; and so on. Many teachers have found that students respond better to homework that is *social* (i.e. that involves them in interacting with other people) rather than *solitary*.

- Experiment with how homework is organised. For example, you could give students a list of things for homework from which they can choose. You could sometimes ask them to tell you what they are going to do for homework, and get them to put it in writing.
- You could involve the students in monitoring their own homework: what they did, when they did it, where they did it, what they found difficult, and how well they performed. You can then see in what circumstances they appear to do best.

AtoZ IDEAS LIST

See **HELP YOURSELF LIST**.

AtoZ INDUCTIVE GRAMMAR

What and why?

GRAMMAR may be approached in two main ways: *deductively*, where students are given a rule which they then practise (that is, they work using other people's deductions about the language), or *inductively*, where they work out rules for themselves. Inductive grammar teaching is useful for a number of reasons. It can involve the students more fully as thinking people with ideas of their own and thus increase motivation. It can involve them more fully in understanding the language as they work out different rules for forming and using English. It can also help clear up misconceptions they have and make it clear to you, the teacher, what ideas they have about how grammar works. *CEWw* includes a number of inductive grammar tasks in the *Language focus* sections.

Practical ideas

- Some aspects of English grammar may be similar in the students' **MOTHER TONGUE**. Students can be asked to think about how things are expressed in their mother tongue and when they use certain words, etc. before they are asked to think about English.
- Students can be given simple tables and asked to complete them (for example, sentences with 'don't' and 'doesn't' missing). They can then look through the Unit in the book to discover which word belongs with which subject pronoun.
- Students can briefly work in small groups/pairs to work out a rule before you ask for their ideas. If their ideas are incorrect, you can then present the correct rule or give some more examples which make them think about the rule further.

AtoZ INSIDE THE TEXT

What and why?

From *CEWw 3* onwards, most of the **READING** texts in the *Topic* and *Language* Units are accompanied by brief tasks which require the students to have a 'global understanding'. For example, a task might ask them to explain in their own words what some key terms from the text mean. The purpose in keeping these tasks brief is to maintain interest and motivation, without making students work out the detail of every text they read. However, it is often important and useful to focus on the vocabulary, grammar and form of a text, so for this reason optional *Inside the text* tasks are provided in the first *Topic* and *Language* Unit in each Theme. *Inside the text* tasks are also provided in the *Out and about* sections.

Practical ideas

- If your class has students of **MIXED ABILITIES**, you can divide the students into different groups. Some students can get extra practice by working through the *Inside the text* tasks, while other students work on freer tasks. (See *Mixed abilities* suggestions in the Unit notes in the Teacher's Book.)
- Students can also make up *Inside the text* tasks for each other, using the ones in the book as examples. Encourage them to look at *Inside the text* exercises in other *Topic* and *Language* Units for ideas.
- The *Help yourself list* at the back of the Student's Book also gives more ideas for *Inside the text* exercises that you or your students can devise. You can put these exercises in a class **EXERCISE BOX**.

A to Z INTERACTIVE WRITING

What and why?

Most often, the writing that students do in school is simply for the eyes of the teacher. Interactive writing involves students writing *to* and *with* other students. There are a number of reasons why this might be useful. Firstly, writing to other students can give the students a clear sense of purpose and a sense of having an audience for their writing – they can get **FEEDBACK** from the reader on how far their message has been understood. Secondly, writing with other students can give them a clear focus for their work. Interactive writing will involve them in asking each other about grammar, spelling, vocabulary, phrasing, etc. and so give them the chance to learn in a non-threatening atmosphere. This kind of interaction is also central to **PROCESS WRITING**.

Practical ideas

- While students are working in groups, you can circulate around the class, reading what they have written and helping with any problems.
- Discussion during interactive writing tasks may be in the **MOTHER TONGUE**. This may not be a problem since one of the purposes of interactive writing is to enable students to exchange ideas. An 'English only' rule may prevent this. The important point is to insist that the writing that they produce is in English.
- Writing can be a sensitive area and some students may not want to write with other students or have their work seen by other students. In this case, they should be entitled to work alone if they wish.

A to Z LANGUAGE RECORD

What and why?

One of the most important and useful tools in learning a language is a personal record of what you have learned. A written record enables students to look back on what they have done in class and refresh their memories. It also encourages them to make sure that they have a clear understanding.

In early levels of *CEWw*, the Student's Book contains *Language Record* pages where students could make a note of the meaning of words and the grammar/functions they learned. From *CEWw 3* onwards, this idea is taken further and students build up their own personal record in a separate notebook.

Practical ideas

- You can decide with the students what word groups they would like to build up in their notebook. Word groups are groups of words around a common topic. For example, they could have a page entitled 'Names of clothes' or 'Words connected with school'.
- The *Vocabulary maps* (*CEWw 3* and onwards) give an example of how word groups can be organised.
- As students finish their work in the *Topic* and *Language* Units, or if they have **TIME TO SPARE**, you can direct them to work on their *Language Record*.
- Initially, you can allow time in class for students to work on their *Language Record*, so that you can check that they have a clear understanding of how it works. Later, they can also work on it for **HOMEWORK**.
- While they are working on the *Language Record*, you can go round **MONITORING AND GUIDING**.

A to Z LEARNING STRATEGIES

What and why?

Learning strategies are the techniques individual students use to help themselves learn. Classroom research has identified three main types of strategies: *meta-cognitive* strategies, such as planning, evaluating and monitoring language use; *cognitive* strategies used in actually 'doing the learning', such as guessing words, repeating, learning things by heart, and working out rules; and *social* strategies, such as working with others, asking for help and so on. All students come to their English lessons with their own learning strategies. They learn many of these through their other schoolwork, through watching people, and by being told what to do. Learning strategies are very personal – what works for one person may not work for another. Since the strategies students use are influenced by teaching and by others, students may not be using the best strategies for *them*. Teaching tends to emphasise particular approaches to learning (e.g. an emphasis on 'item' level exercises such as gap-fill, matching, etc.). Students are unlikely to be aware of what the alternatives might be and may assume that the way they learn and are taught is the only way.

Learning about learning is part of the process of education and provides an understanding which is transferable to other subjects, other areas of life and beyond school. It is also important in bringing about **STUDENT INVOLVEMENT**.

EVALUATION sections also ask students to think about – and discuss – how they learn.

Practical ideas

- *CEWw* includes exercises which use various kinds of learning strategies. Meta-cognitive strategies are involved in the DECIDE ... exercises, in exercises which include a DO IT YOURSELF element, and in the HELP YOURSELF section in the Workbook. *Cognitive* strategies are developed all through the Student's Book and are supported by the HELP YOURSELF LIST (or *Ideas list*). *Social* strategies are involved in the numerous groupwork and individual tasks, the encouragement to ask others and share ideas, and to use resources from outside the classroom.
- Before giving a test, discuss with the students *how* they will revise.
- When they choose a DECIDE ... exercise, ask them why they chose *that* one.
- You could make a POSTER with ideas from the students about how they revise for tests, how they do their HOMEWORK, how they check their work, what they do to learn English in their free time, and so on.
- There are few 'right' or 'wrong' ways to learn a language. Some students may feel happier, for example, looking at a model before they write, while others prefer to 'write from the top of their heads'. The important point is that students are aware of the possibilities. Every now and again, discuss with the students how they are going to do an exercise and allow a variety of learning approaches. In some cases, this may include looking at the answers *first,* for example.

Researching the classroom

Learning strategies generally take place inside the students' heads, so it is very difficult to find out precisely what strategies they are using. However, there are ways to get a better picture and to determine if students are using the most effective strategies.

- At the end of each lesson ask students to note down (in the mother tongue) what they thought the main point of the lesson was, what they learnt from the lesson, which exercise helped them the most/least and what they found easiest/most difficult. Collect in the papers. This will give you an idea of what *they* focus on. This may not be the same as what you think is important. (For example, one teacher who did this after a 'grammar lesson', found that the students actually thought the lesson was about 'vocabulary'. In such cases, it's not surprising that the students don't learn the key grammar points.) If this is the situation in your class, you may find it useful to discuss it with the students.
- As part of their homework, ask students to write down exactly *what* they did, how they approached it, where they did their homework, who with, what they used (dictionary, cassette, a friend, etc.) to help them complete it. Collect in their papers.
- You can prepare a brief questionnaire to find out what your students do when they are learning. For example: (i) What makes it easier for you to understand the cassette?; (ii) When you are reading in English and you see a new word, what do you do?; (iii) How do you revise for a test?; (iv) How do you remember English spelling?
- A better idea might be to ask the students to design a questionnaire for another class, perhaps called 'How do you learn?'. This will not only give the students very useful language practice, but will also tell you a lot about what *they* think is important.
- Watch them! After you have set the students working, watch what they do. You could focus on one or two students and notice the steps that they go through, what seems to be slowing them down or helping them, and so about. Afterwards, you could start a general discussion on this.

A to Z LISTENING

What and why?

In common with the other skills of WRITING, READING and SPEAKING, there are two main roles for listening in language teaching. The first is as a *goal* of learning. It is important for students to develop the listening skill in order to understand spoken English, whether on TV, on radio or in speaking to people. The second role, however, is as a *means* of learning. Listening can provide further sources of input and can help the students remember the words, phrases, grammar, etc. that they are learning. By working on listening tasks, students can become closely involved with the language and, in doing so, develop their general language proficiency. Handled well, listening can thus form a very important element in the course.

Practical ideas

- In the early stages, the emphasis is probably best placed on listening as a *means* of learning rather than as a *goal* of learning. This means that rather than treating listening as 'comprehension' exercises, students can listen to texts they have read and discussed as a way of consolidating their learning. They can also look at the text while they are listening.
- For listening to work well, students have to be able to hear! If you are in a noisy classroom, close doors, windows, turn off fans, etc. while you are playing the cassette.
- With larger classes, students can listen in smaller groups while the other students are doing something else.

- Unless you are conducting a test, you can allow the students to listen again if they wish or to pause the tape to check the meaning. Listening in this case will be useful for learning English generally.
- Control of the cassette player can be passed to a student. Other students may then feel freer to ask for things to be replayed or paused.

- Before the end of a lesson, you can play the listening passage again as a way of recapping what you have done.
- If the students are doing a listening comprehension exercise, they can work in pairs with one of the students listening for answers to some of the questions and the other student listening for answers to the other questions. They can then compare afterwards.

AtoZ MEMORY

What and why?

Memory is obviously crucial in language learning. How memory comes about, however, is still something of a mystery to us. We know that the memories which last the longest are often complete experiences – research has also shown, for example, that many language learners are able to say when they first heard a word and describe the scene at the time: where they were, what the weather was like, what they were doing and so on.

In practice, we can think of two basic ways to bring about memorisation. One is through rote learning, that is, 'learning by heart'. The other is through 'activation', that is, through *use* or building connections with other knowledge and experiences. In the past, much language learning concentrated almost solely on rote learning: students were encouraged to learn words, phrases and dialogues by heart, often without fully understanding them. This approach has been heavily criticised in recent years, but there are benefits in *some* rote learning. Where, for example, we need frequent mental reference to 'fixed' information – such as multiplication tables in mathematics or irregular verbs in a foreign language – it may be efficient to learn by heart. Secondly, it is often psychologically comforting at any age to learn a piece of text (for example, a poem or a song) by heart, particularly if this is done in a group.

The benefits of rote learning, however, are quite different from those achieved through 'activation' – that is, the use of language in a variety of contexts to express and understand meanings, particularly those that are *significant* to the student, with a variety of TASKS. Memory achieved through activation is usually transferable to other contexts; memory achieved through rote learning generally has a more limited value. Rote learning is more effective for short-term memory needs but retention rapidly falls. After one year, as much as 75% of rote-learned information is beyond recall. Long-term memory requires understanding, frequent revision, personal involvement and varied opportunities for use and application. In language learning, it is VOCABULARY which makes most demands on memory.

Practical ideas

- The HELP YOURSELF section in the Workbook includes ideas on improving memory.

- You can encourage students to think about what kind of memory they have: some remember images well, others remember spoken or written text, some may remember smells or bodily experience well. You can ask the students to picture in their mind an event in the recent past when they heard people talking. Ask them to write down anything they remember about it: the weather, the room, the clothes, the words people said, what they could smell, how they felt, etc. Their memories will give clues as to the kind of memoriser they are and the kinds of LEARNING STRATEGIES they will be able to use to help them remember new information. Students who remember visual details may well find it helpful to visualise new words in a picture or film. Those who remember verbal details – what people said, for example – may memorise new words best by fitting them into a narrative.
- You can ask students to experiment with the ways they use their LANGUAGE RECORD. The words can be written in different coloured pens: red may be more memorable than blue, for example. Or they can be written in different shapes: words about 'the environment' may, for example, be written on a globe; words about 'the news' could be written on a TV screen.
- You can ask students to classify words in different ways: putting nouns, verbs, adjectives in separate lists or in alphabetical order, or making lists of opposites, or putting the short words first and then the long ones.
- Students can also experiment by writing the words in different places: in their diary, on the back of an envelope, on a postcard, on the side of a cardboard box, on a bus ticket or chocolate wrapper.
- The place of learning might also be important: students can experiment with learning language in different places: in different rooms of the house, or outside, in a busy café or a quiet library.
- You can also encourage students to build learning into a 'complete event'. For example, if they are trying to revise for a test they can play some MUSIC at the same time. Later, if they listen to the music it may help to bring the ideas back to them.
- Some students like rhymes. Learning new words can be helped by rhyming them with a word they already know.

- Encourage students to create different ways of using new words while and after they learn them: by writing a puzzle or recording a dialogue on the tape or writing a letter.
- Allow time in class to discuss the different experiments the students have carried out so that they can evaluate their successes and failures.

- An experiment that you can try is to give the same vocabulary test again later in the term or even in the next term and see which words have been remembered best. Then discuss with the students why some words are more easily remembered than others.

AtoZ MIXED ABILITIES

What and why?

All classes are 'mixed ability' classes. All classes consist of individual students with different personalities and interests. All students also, themselves, have 'mixed abilities'. For example, some students may find writing easier than speaking, or vice versa. Some students find one particular task or approach more appealing than other tasks or approaches. It is also important to distinguish two aspects of 'ability': language ability and language-learning ability. The first aspect refers to how much language the students actually know/understand at a particular point in time. The second aspect refers to their ability to learn. A student may be weak in English, for example, but given appropriate support may be able to learn quickly. This suggests that some 'mixed ability' classes may be the result of particular approaches to teaching (the ability to learn or the ability to be taught?). For this reason, teachers need to adopt a flexible methodology that allows for a variety of learning styles and abilities (see **LEARNING STRATEGIES**).

Practical ideas

- One key principle in teaching mixed ability groups is *transparency*. Try to make sure that *all* students understand what is happening in the lesson, for example by **OVERVIEWING** before beginning a lesson or a new task.
- There are a number of ways in which you can approach teaching groups of mixed language and learning ability: (1) stronger/average/weaker students can be given completely different tasks at different levels of difficulty; (2) students can be given tasks on the same topic at varying levels of difficulty (see below); (3) students can be involved in **OPEN-ENDED TASKS** which allow them to respond at their own level of ability. In principle, approaches (2) and (3) are better, since they avoid students feeling left out. Approach (3), additionally, allows students to develop more freely without being restricted by the tasks themselves.
- To provide tasks at varying levels of difficulty on the same topic, text, etc., think about how a task can be made more challenging or how more support can be given. In the teaching notes for most of the Units there are ideas for making these kinds of adjustments to the key exercises in the Units.
- At the back of the Teacher's Books, there are additional photocopiable *Language worksheets* for each grammar point in the *Topic* and *Language* Units.
- The **TIME TO SPARE?** exercises at the end of each *Topic* and *Language* Unit provide further tasks for varying levels of ability.
- **DECIDE … EXERCISES** encourage students to make choices about what they need to do and to work at their own pace.
- In **GROUPWORK**, try to mix students so that students of all abilities can work together.
- See further ideas under **LISTENING**, **SPEAKING**, **READING** and **WRITING**.

AtoZ MONITORING AND GUIDING

What and why?

In many of the activities in *CEWw*, students will be working in small groups or pairs. This way of working has many advantages, in that it gives students a chance to work at their own pace, to ask each other for help, to share ideas and to get more language practice. **GROUPWORK** and **PAIRWORK**, however, can run the danger of students wasting their time together as they become distracted, talk about or do things other than requested, or produce work which is full of errors. For this reason, monitoring and guiding by the teacher are very important.

Practical ideas

- Before setting students to work in pairs/groups, check that they understand fully what they are going to do. You can go through one or two examples with the whole class first.
- While they are working, go round the class. You can check whether they are having any problems, check the work they have done, give extra ideas where necessary, and generally keep them on the task.
- While going round the class, you can also note down common errors that you notice. You can then spend a short time at the end of the lesson, going through a few of these.

- You can also make a note of which students seem to be working well together and which seem to be having problems. Next time, you can vary the way you set up **GROUPWORK** accordingly.

- Before students start working, you can put some **TASKS IN BLOCKS**. When students have finished the work, they can move on to something from the **EXERCISE BOX**, look back at previous Units, or choose a **DO IT YOURSELF** task.

AtoZ MOTHER TONGUE

What and why?

The mother tongue plays an important role in all language learning. Firstly, it is an important tool for the teacher to clarify explanations, give instructions and provide translations. In many cases, a brief explanation in the mother tongue can lead to a more efficient use of classroom time. Secondly, the mother tongue is itself a primary learning tool. As with all other kinds of learning, a large part of language learning involves relating what you are learning to what you already know, in this case the mother tongue. Studies show that all students, even advanced level students, use the mother tongue as a resource consciously and subconsciously in language learning activities and in natural language use. Thus, the tasks and activities in *CEWw* provide opportunities for the students to compare with their mother tongue and at times to plan things in the mother tongue. Comparison with the mother tongue can help to ensure that the *correct* meanings are learned.

Practical ideas

- Students may also use the mother tongue because they feel embarrassed about speaking English in front of the whole class. In these cases, you can give them time to prepare what they are going to say (see **PROCESSING TIME**).

- If you feel the students use too much of the mother tongue (for example, in groupwork), you will need to consider why this situation is arising and what you can do about it. It may be that the task is too difficult for them, not interesting enough, not clear to them or too unstructured. You could try to discuss the problem with them, give clear examples of what they have to do or ask for suggestions from them.

- From *CEWw 2* onwards, you should be able to use English for most of your classroom management, and you can encourage (or require) the students to reply to you in English.

- You will need to decide *when* you will use the mother tongue. You might, for example, limit yourself to explanations of grammar and vocabulary and to when you are **MONITORING AND GUIDING**.

- You will also need to decide when you will accept the mother tongue from the students. For example, you may accept use of the mother tongue in brainstorming activities in which you translate their ideas and put them on the board.

AtoZ MOTIVATION

What and why?

Of all the different factors involved in language learning, motivation is probably one of the most important. Researchers have suggested that there are two main types of motivation in language learning: *instrumental* – which means that people study in order to use the language (e.g. in their work) – and *integrative* – which means that they study because they want to know more about a foreign language culture. With young learners, neither of these types of motivation is generally relevant. There is often very little immediate need to learn the language and it is probably unlikely that they are particularly attracted to a foreign language culture. This means that many teachers feel they have to resort to other ways to motivate their students, using songs, games, fun activities and texts that appeal to their interests. This can be very exhausting. Many teachers complain that they feel they have to 'entertain' their students in order to 'make' them learn.

A contrasting view is that motivation is not something that comes from *outside* the students. It is something *inside* them, which the teacher has to try to 'open up'. Rather than trying to find endless ways to 'entertain' the students, the teacher looks for ways to bring about a deeper, more enduring sense of **STUDENT INVOLVEMENT**, through such things as **OPEN-ENDED TASKS**. Teachers who think this way start from the assumption that the vast majority of people naturally want to learn, if they are given the right conditions, and what often kills motivation is forcing things on people. They also think that people naturally want to assume responsibility for their own lives, and look for ways to support this in the language classroom. The more they are involved in deciding what they will do, the more 'ownership' and personal involvement they have.

Practical ideas

- If the students do not seem very motivated to do a particular task, ask yourself why. What is it about the situation that makes them unmotivated?

- Don't expect constant motivation! Everybody has ups and downs – there are many other things happening in the students' lives and their English classes are just a small part of it.

- If motivation seems to be a particular problem, perhaps you can discuss it with the students. Ask them what they find uninteresting about their work – perhaps it's too difficult, too easy, too similar to other work they have been doing.
- Try to think positively about all the students. Assume first that they will succeed and encourage them. If the students think that you will expect them to fail, they probably will!
- Try to set **OPEN-ENDED TASKS** which you know that all students will be able to do at their level of ability rather than setting tasks which you know will generate failure. Many of these may involve students in **PROBLEM SOLVING**.

- Build in opportunities for individual students to be occasional 'experts' on something: students may have an interesting hobby or collection or may have spent time overseas, or perhaps you could ask a student to find out more about a certain subject and then tell the class about it.
- Give the students opportunities to take responsibility for things and to be involved in fundamental, important decisions about their work – for example, to be involved in designing tests, in the **EVALUATION** of their work, and in **DO IT YOURSELF** tasks. Try to develop the students' **AUTONOMY**.

A to Z MUSIC

What and why?

Potentially, music can have an important role in the classroom. The use of **SONGS** is already very familiar to most teachers. Music, however, plays a major role in many parts of our lives. We may, for example, listen to the radio while we are working, while we are driving or waiting for something. There may be background music while we are eating or reading. We may use music to relax or to mark a change of activity (such as 'coming home from work') and so on. In similar ways, music can be used to help make the classroom more welcoming.

Practical ideas

- Choose music for the atmosphere you want to create: soft calm music if you want to calm the students down, energetic music if you want to wake them up, and so on.
- You can play music as they come into the classroom. This can help 'bring them into' English again, and relax them ready for work.
- You could use music regularly at set phases in your teaching – for example, when they are writing, doing short exercises or doing an *Activity* Unit. Students could then suggest or bring in appropriate pieces of music.
- If there are a number of steps or phases in an activity, you can use music to mark the transition. For example, some fast music for a **BRAINSTORMING** phase and a slow, gentle piece of music for a writing phase.

A to Z OPEN-ENDED TASKS

What and why?

Open-ended tasks are tasks to which there is not a single absolutely correct answer or where a variety of answers are possible. They can be distinguished from 'closed tasks', where students have to answer in a particular way. An example of an open-ended task might be where the students are asked to imagine a person standing in a pair of shoes which they are shown and then to write a description of that person. A closed task using the same type of language might be one where they are given a description with certain words missing, which they have to supply. Both closed tasks and open-ended tasks are useful in language teaching. Where students are working in groups, for example, closed tasks can force the students to discuss more in order to find the correct answer. Open-ended tasks, however, are also very valuable for a number of reasons. Since there is no single correct answer, the students can often answer at the level of their ability. This means that in classes with **MIXED ABILITIES**, students can be working on the same tasks at the same time. Open-ended tasks also allow for more **STUDENT INVOLVEMENT** since the students are asked to contribute more of their own personal

ideas. This means that the outcome of classroom work will be richer – there will be a variety of ideas expressed which students can further compare and discuss. In this way, the students' **AUTONOMY** in their own use of English can be developed. Open-ended tasks also allow you, the teacher, to get a good idea of what the students are capable of producing.

For some further examples of open and closed tasks, see the **HELP YOURSELF LIST** in the Student's Book from Level 3 onwards.

Practical ideas

- If, at the start of a course, you are uncertain how much English the students know, you can use an open-ended task to help you find out. See the *Help yourself list* in the Student's Book (*CEWw 3* onwards) for some ideas.
- You can set the students some open-ended writing tasks by asking them to write their ideas about some educationally broad **QUESTIONS**, particularly ones which require **PROBLEM SOLVING**.
- The students' answers to open-ended tasks can be included in a **PARCEL OF ENGLISH**. They will give the

school or class that you send the parcel to a good idea of the range of abilities and interests in your class.

- Instead of asking the students conventional 'closed' comprehension questions about a text they have listened to or read, you can ask open-ended questions. For

example, you can ask 'What do you think about …?', 'What would you do …?', 'Do you think it was good that …?', 'Why do you think he/she did that?', 'What do you think they said to each other?', 'What do you think he/she was thinking?' and so on.

AtoZ OVERVIEWING

What and why?

A common experience of some students is that they often do not have a very clear sense of where they are in a lesson – they may have very little idea of what has just happened, an unclear idea of what they are supposed to be doing now, and no idea at all of what is going to happen next. As one teacher put it, for many students being in a classroom is rather like being put in a taxi without being told where you are going or what landmarks to look out for on the way. Overviewing is a technique which helps to give students a clearer idea of where they are in the lesson. That way, if they lose concentration for a short time, they won't lose their grip on the whole lesson (100% concentration during a whole 40–50 minute lesson requires a lot of mental effort!).

Practical ideas

- Before the students begin a new Theme, you can ask them to find certain things in the Units that follow – for example, a photograph of something, an exercise that practises a particular grammar point, or a text about a particular topic. The Teacher's Book will give you ideas for these introductory tasks.
- Before moving into an activity which has several steps, you can give the students an overview of what they will be doing. It will then be easier to move them on from one step to the next, once the activity has begun.
- You can place an overview of the lesson on the board at the start of the lesson, showing what they will be doing.
- You can give an overview of your next lesson, leaving open some period of time. Students can then be asked to suggest ideas of things they would like to do (you could use a Suggestion Box for this). This will help create a feeling of **STUDENT INVOLVEMENT** in the lesson. (Have something planned, just in case!)

AtoZ PACE

What and why?

The **TIMING** and pace of any lesson are linked together. Timing is concerned with the management of the time available for each class, that is, *when* certain things happen. Pace is more concerned with the rate at which the students work. All students work at a different pace and they thus need to be allowed to work at a rate at which they feel comfortable. *CEWw* provides a number of ways of preventing some students from falling behind because the pace is too fast and of preventing others from getting bored because the pace is too slow.

Different types of classroom activities will naturally have a different pace. For example, oral discussion with the whole class may be experienced as 'faster' than individual writing. **PAIRWORK** may be experienced as more relaxed than questions and answers with the teacher. These differences in pace can be used to give variety to the shape of the lesson and thus sustain interest.

Practical ideas

- In large classes with **MIXED ABILITIES**, different students can work on different tasks at the same time at their own pace.
- For most of the exercises, except the initial **BRAINSTORMING** and **OVERVIEWING** ones, students can work at their own pace (see **MONITORING AND GUIDING**).
- Certain parts of the course will allow students more opportunity to have direct control over their learning and thus their pace: the **TIME TO SPARE?** sections, the **EXERCISE BOX**, the **DECIDE … EXERCISES** and the use of **GROUPWORK** and **PAIRWORK**.
- If certain students are working at a very slow pace, you will need to ask yourself why this is and if you can or should do anything about it. For example, they may be tired, they may be confused, they may not understand the task, they may be bored, they may have things on their mind. You will then need to decide if you should intervene – for example, by encouraging them to work faster or by explaining things to them again.

AtoZ PAIRWORK

What and why?

Pairwork involves students working in pairs simultaneously. The reasons for the use of pairwork are similar to those of **GROUPWORK**. Pairwork allows more students to get more practice. It also provides a change of pace to a lesson and helps to sustain motivation. Students working in pairs are able to share ideas and help each other. However, pairwork can fail if it is not set up well. This can lead to students getting distracted, becoming disenchanted with English and, eventually, misbehaving.

Practical ideas

- Ensure that students know exactly what they have to do before they begin any pairwork activity. Run through a few examples with the whole class. Initially at least,

pairwork tasks need to have a clear, concrete focus, for example on completing an exercise, doing **PATTERNED PRACTICE**, preparing some **INTERACTIVE WRITING**, preparing questions and so on.
- For variety, different students can be paired together. Students can be moved around the room or they can be put into pairs with students to their left or right, in front or behind.
- Give the students a time limit so that they know when they have to finish.
- Students can work in pairs to produce questions, exercises, etc. for other pairs to do.
- If the task does not actually *require* pairwork, the students can choose whether they want to work in pairs or alone.

AtoZ PARCEL OF ENGLISH

What and why?

A *Parcel of English* is a collection of pieces of work which the students can produce and send to another class (perhaps in another country) or display in their school. Supplementary

Unit A shows students what they can put in a *Parcel of English*. Cambridge University Press offers a link-up scheme for classes to make contact with classes in other countries of the world. For further details see the Teacher's Books for *CEWw*.

AtoZ PARTICIPATION

What and why?

Particularly in large classes, some students may seem reluctant to participate orally and contribute to the lessons. There may be a number of reasons for this. There may, for example, be a number of negative factors such as being afraid to make mistakes in front of others, feeling that they will appear stupid, fearing that they will be corrected, or otherwise lacking in confidence in front of a large group. On the other hand, many students naturally say very little. They may feel that they learn best through listening and observing – silence is their preferred **LEARNING STRATEGY**. Before you insist on students participating orally in the lesson, it is best therefore to think about *why* they are not participating. What may seem a problem to you may not, in fact, be a problem to them. It is important to respect the personal preferences that different students may have. There are, however, a number of things that you can do to improve the chances of students participating.

Practical ideas

- If there are one or two students that are persistently quiet, you could talk to them after a lesson to find out what they think about it. Alternatively, you could make up a questionnaire which *all* students can answer.
- If possible, try to arrange the seating so that all the students can see you clearly and so that they can see each other.

A horseshoe arrangement or circle is best, or try and push the desks together into pairs or groups.
- Accept that some students are quiet and may feel happier contributing in a less obvious way – perhaps by producing exercises and puzzles for a class **EXERCISE BOX**, or helping to organise the **PARCEL OF ENGLISH**, or bringing in pictures and 'realia' for other activities.
- Some students may dominate the class by being over-noisy or always answering questions first. If this is a problem, you could divide the class into four quarters and say that you will accept an answer from each group in turn.
- Some students may be reluctant to 'act out' in class. They may prefer to record a conversation on cassette at home for you to listen to later. Don't force students to speak out loud if they are not willing or ready.
- Make sure that the students understand that many of the activities in *CEWw* are open-ended so that a variety of answers are acceptable and 'right'. It is what *they* think that is important.
- Encourage students to understand the importance of everyone's contribution in **GROUPWORK** and that the work that the quiet students do often supports the work of the more dominant ones.
- Allow students to work at their own **PACE** (see also **TASKS IN BLOCKS**). This will give the more apprehensive students an opportunity to work without pressure.

- The **DECIDE … EXERCISES** also allow students freedom to choose what they prefer to do. Give the quieter students encouragement while they work, to build up confidence.

- You could make a particular point of praising weaker or quieter students and of accepting what they say (even if this contains many errors) in an effort to build up their confidence.

AtoZ PATTERN PRACTICE

What and why?

A key part of language learning is having the opportunity to use the language creatively to say real things. However, there is also an element in language learning which involves practising particular structures or forms so that students can produce them effortlessly. One way in which this can be done is through pattern practice. Students produce sentences following a particular pattern and in doing so develop their ability to control the mechanical aspects of language production. Over-used, however, pattern practice can produce students who become bored and who find it difficult to use the language to actually communicate. For this reason, *CEWw* includes relatively few patterned exercises.

Practical ideas

- Pattern practice exercises can be done in small groups or pairs so that students get more opportunity to speak without having to wait for the rest of the class.
- The focus of pattern practice activities is on the *form* of what is said. This is the appropriate time to ensure that things are said accurately.
- Before getting students to work in pairs/groups on a patterned exercise, go through a few examples with the whole class so they know what is expected.
- While they are working, you can be **MONITORING AND GUIDING**.
- Oral pattern practice exercises can also be done in writing.

AtoZ PHYSICAL MOVEMENT

What and why?

In school, students may often spend many hours confined to a desk as they have one lesson then another. This can lead to boredom and restlessness (with its effect on **DISCIPLINE**). Physical movement can also be important for other reasons. If students can be physically involved with English, it can lead to deeper, more long-lasting learning as the language becomes more 'concrete' to them and involves them as whole persons. Adolescent students, however, are often very self-conscious about moving around in the classroom (as are many adults) so it is important to choose activities carefully. Many games that work successfully with younger students may appear 'childish' to adolescent students.

Practical ideas

- 'Simon says' games, in which students have to carry out actions upon the orders of the teacher/a student work successfully with younger students but may not be acceptable to older students.
- 'Total physical response' activities, however, can work well if they are approached seriously (at first). They are probably more useful in teaching beginning students, however, with the teacher saying a verb and the students doing the action.
- It may be possible to involve more physical movement simply by moving to another place. It may, for example, be possible to have the English lesson outside in a playground or in the hall, where the students will be standing up. This is especially useful if you want to do a **ROLE PLAY** with the students, or if they are working on **POSTERS**.

- If you are **DISPLAYING STUDENTS' WORK** you can put it up in different parts of the room so that students have to move around to look at it.
- A 'cocktail party' activity is also useful for getting the students to move. Students can move around the classroom talking to other students, perhaps trying to find some information. For example, you could pin the name of a country on the back of each student. That student must then ask other students questions to discover what country it is. They can only ask one question before they move to another student and they can only reply 'yes' or 'no' to a question.
- Students can represent something in a group. For example, they might together form the shape of their country. They can then move to where they would like to be in their country and talk about why they want to go there. They could ask each other across the map: 'Peter, where are you?' 'I'm in Barcelona, in the north-east.' Students can similarly form maps of their town, maps of a jungle and maps of their school.
- Mime is also useful. Students act out a word and the others have to guess what it is.
- You could have various items of clothing available such as hats, gloves, etc. to make roundelays, acting out, mime, etc. more fun.
- Physical activity doesn't have to be related to language learning. You might start a lesson or break up a long lesson by getting the students to do something, for example, shake their arms, stand up and turn round a few times or walk around the room. You could combine this with **MUSIC**.

AtoZ POSTERS

What and why?

At various places in *CEWw*, students are required to produce posters of their ideas. The production of posters is a useful technique in language teaching for a number of reasons. It gives the students a concrete focus for their work and also ensures that English (rather than only the MOTHER TONGUE) is produced as a result of their GROUPWORK. Poster production can also be a lively way of working. Students can design their posters, spend time on how they look and express their ideas graphically. Poster production can form a welcome break from a linear presentation of ideas in which groups FEEDBACK, one after the other, to the whole class. Posters allow all groups to FEEDBACK simultaneously, thus using time more effectively. They also form a permanent record of the work that has been done that can be DISPLAYED.

Practical ideas

- For poster production you – or the students – will need to have available supplies of large sheets of paper, coloured pens, scissors, glue or adhesive tape, and something to fix the posters to the wall.
- Coloured sheets mounted on a white background can make posters more attractive to look at.
- Students can be asked to work on parts of their posters for HOMEWORK, once they have decided in their group what they want to write.
- Encourage them to produce a draft before they put their writing on a poster.
- Once the students are ready with their posters, you can put them up on the wall or lay them out on the desks. Students can then walk around the class, looking at the posters. You could ask one member of each group to stay by their poster to explain what they have done.
- Posters can be photographed for permanent reference. A class photograph can be taken with their poster display.

AtoZ PROBLEM SOLVING

What and why?

Learning how to approach and solve problems, and accepting that there is often more than one answer to a question or more than one way of dealing with it, is a key part of both education and language learning. The ability to determine the essence of a problem, and indeed to see that there *is* a problem, is a vital ingredient in learning. In *CEWw*, therefore, many tasks require the students to think things through not only in relation to the structure of the language but also by drawing on their existing knowledge to help them understand new situations. For example, some exercises in which the students are asked to establish their own rules for a new grammatical structure require this kind of cognitive effort. Other exercises require students to think through *why* certain things happen, or to work out an explanation for natural phenomena.

The benefits of a problem-solving approach to teaching and learning can be significant for a number of reasons. Firstly, involving the learner in thinking things through requires more involvement and produces greater depth of understanding. This kind of 'experiential knowledge' (that is, the knowledge gained through the experience of *doing* something) often lasts longer and is more significant to the learner than knowledge which is simply 'transmitted' by the teacher or the book. The students become involved in constructing their own *individual* systems of learning and understanding. Secondly, some recent research has suggested that where students are involved in using language to understand and formulate meanings, language may be acquired more naturally, in much the same way as infants learn their first language.

Practical ideas

- When students ask you questions, you can, from time to time, insist that they find out for themselves by using books, asking other people or figuring it out.
- Give hints or clues rather than direct answers.
- You can set a 'problem of the week' for the students. Talk to other subject teachers in your school and ask for ideas about questions you could pose. 'What if …' questions and 'How can …' questions are often useful in stimulating thought. For example: 'What would happen if we had only three hours of light each day?', 'What would happen if we started teaching Chinese instead of English in school?', 'How can we make our classroom lighter and quieter?' Even: 'How can we best learn a language?' If you set such questions, you can discuss them at a specified time later.
- You can present 'language learning' as a 'problem' to be solved. Encourage students to think of their own ways of recording and learning new vocabulary. Let students discuss and compare in class the different methods they have tried. Encourage students to discuss grammar areas which they find difficult or easy to learn and use. Encourage the students to think about and investigate *how* they go about doing exercises, reading, how they revise for a test, etc.
- Students can be encouraged to bring puzzles and problems into class. They can also put these into the EXERCISE BOX and the PARCEL OF ENGLISH.

AtoZ PROCESSING TIME

What and why?

Learning – whether it is a foreign language or any other subject – often requires great mental effort. In any 40–50 minute lesson, a student may be required to absorb a lot of new information, to connect it to what he or she already knows, and then to use it. Each of these processes takes time. Often, when students are asked a question and fail to answer correctly, the problem is not that they don't know or haven't understood, it is simply that they haven't been given enough time to process the question and process an answer. If students are questioned with the whole class listening and waiting, there may be pressure on them to answer as quickly as possible. This can block their ability to process the question and an answer – that is, to think. The teacher may then feel under pressure to keep the lesson moving and so turns to another student. The same situation may repeat itself several times, until finally, a student who has not been put under this direct pressure, and who has thus had enough time to process the question, is able to produce a satisfactory answer. This problem may be avoided by allowing all students processing time before you call for answers.

Practical ideas

- Allow students time to do an exercise by themselves / in pairs before you call for answers.
- Give students time to plan out in writing what they are going to say, their ideas on a topic, etc. before you discuss things with the whole class.
- Tell the students in advance what they will be doing. They can then prepare at home for the lesson.
- Choose 'larger' tasks which can be done in a large space of time (such as the majority of tasks in *CEWw*) rather than short 'item' tasks which require immediate responses (such as comprehension questions, gap-fill exercises).

AtoZ PROCESS WRITING

What and why?

The English author E. M. Forster once said 'How can I know what I think until I see what I say?' By this, he meant that it was only through trying to get his ideas on to paper that he could discover what his ideas were. Recent research into **WRITING** has confirmed this: 'good writers' do not simply transfer their ideas from their heads on to paper. The act of writing is also an act of thinking, and writing goes through a process as ideas evolve and change. Rather like working on a sculpture or painting, writing involves putting down a first idea, 'standing back', looking at it and continually rewriting it. Students need to be encouraged to go through these stages, and to look at their writing through the eyes of a reader. They can also gain a lot by seeing writing as a way of helping them develop their own ideas.

Practical ideas

- A process approach to writing involves getting the students to take their writing through different stages: getting ideas, making notes, planning, drafting, getting feedback, revising and finalising. The optional *Activity Units* and creative writing tasks in *CEWw* can be used to encourage students to do this.
- You can also involve students in process writing through **OPEN-ENDED TASKS** which require them to use their imagination. For example, an item of clothing can be used to stimulate the students' imagination and create a story. Similarly, a story can be created around a series of sounds. Students can also be involved in writing poems.
- Students can get a lot of ideas by **BRAINSTORMING** in groups first.
- If you ask the students to produce a longer text, you can put them into writing groups, so that they can get **FEEDBACK** from each other. You can ask the students to spend a fixed amount of time giving feedback on each person's work.
- When students are asked to comment on other students' work, they are often very negative. It is always easy to be negative – you can insist that they have to make positive suggestions.
- You can make **POSTERS** of the students' work, showing the different stages that they have gone through.
- Try to view writing as an opportunity for the students' learning – not just for assessment.
- Writing naturally involves making mistakes, and it is through making mistakes that we learn. You can encourage the students to experiment and 'take risks' with their English, and to try to find ways to express their own ideas.
- If you want to grade some writing, make it clear to the students that the stages that they go through will not be graded and that you will only grade the final piece of work.
- You can also involve students in **EVALUATION** of their own work. You could try to agree with the students what qualities a grade A piece of work would have, then a grade B and so on. They can then compare their own with the grade descriptions.

AtoZ PRONUNCIATION

What and why?

Correct and clear pronunciation is obviously of considerable importance in language learning. Without it, students may not be understood and may be poorly perceived by other English speakers. However, good pronunciation is something which takes time to build up as there are many factors involved. Students need to hear a lot of English before they can develop a 'feel' for the sounds of English. They need to have confidence in their abilities, not feel shy and be ready to make a fool of themselves as they try to get their tongues round the different sounds. Pronunciation is thus probably best dealt with a little at a time and in the context of learning new words, structures, etc. rather than in isolation.

Practical ideas

- In the Listening and Speaking Pack there are *Say it clearly!* exercises which focus on pronunciation work.
- It is better to spend very short periods running through pronunciation examples and exercises rather than one long session. Perhaps the same pronunciation exercise could be done in three or four different lessons for three minutes at a time.
- It is worth discovering which are the main pronunciation problems for students of your **MOTHER TONGUE**. You can then spend a little time focusing on them. A little pronunciation practice goes a long way!
- Students may find stress and intonation practice easier and more interesting to respond to by doing some jazz chants or clapping as the words are stressed on the cassette. This can be done in a small group if they have the cassette recorder or briefly with all the students together.
- Students can be encouraged to do pronunciation work at home. If you go through the *Say it clearly!* exercises with the students, you can ask them to practise again at home.

- **READING** aloud is a technique which is often used to check pronunciation. In our experience, however, reading aloud has very little effect in improving pronunciation. In the classroom, students typically make *more* mistakes when they read aloud than they do normally. It also wastes time for the students who have to listen and places the teacher in the role of having to correct the reader all the time. Turning the written word into sounds is quite a separate process from the production of a word in normal conversation.

Researching the classroom

- Personality and background can have a lot of influence on the way students see themselves as 'English speakers'. This will influence their pronunciation. Try to identify which of your students have the clearest pronunciation in English. Can you explain this in terms of their background or their personality? Do they have certain things in common? Are they, for example, quiet students or more extrovert? Have they travelled to English-speaking countries? Are they musical?
- Some pronunciation problems *may* originate in the difference between sounds in the **MOTHER TONGUE** and sounds in English. Is this true with your students? Can you identify which sounds these are? Try an experiment. Identify two sounds which you know are very different in English from the mother tongue or which don't exist in the students' mother tongue. Give the students explicit practice in one of the sounds but do not pay any special attention to the other sound. After a few weeks, judge how well the students use each sound. Does explicit pronunciation practice always make a difference?

AtoZ QUESTIONS

What and why?

Questions are important in language learning in three main ways. Firstly, and most obviously, the 'interrogative' is a grammatical form which students need to learn to master. For users of a foreign language, the ability to ask questions is essential. It provides the key to moving around in a new environment, integrating into a community and finding essential information. Secondly, questions form one of the main 'tools' which teachers use to check students' comprehension and to get them to produce language. Thirdly, and more profoundly, the ability to generate questions is central to **AUTONOMY** in learning and to the students' personal *educational* development. Many types of questions used in classrooms, however, are *display questions* – that is, they require the students simply to show that they

know something. This places the emphasis on reproducing isolated facts. Educational questions, on the other hand, require the students to think, to discuss, to share ideas or to investigate. They can bring about more **STUDENT INVOLVEMENT** with learning English and with their educational development in general. *CEWw* places particular emphasis on educational questions rather than display questions.

Practical ideas

- When beginning a new topic, you can get students to **BRAINSTORM** what they already know about it and what they would like to find out. You can get the students to produce a question **POSTER** of things they can investigate/research over the next few weeks.

- Where possible, ask **OPEN-ENDED** questions, to which various answers are possible, rather than closed display questions where only one answer is correct. For example, after reading a text, instead of asking factual questions such as 'What did the man do in the shop?' (the answer to which is in the text), you could ask 'What do you think about what he did?', 'Why do you think that?'
- Before reading a text, or after reading part of a text, you can ask the students to predict what will happen next.
- If the students have a reading text with conventional comprehension questions, you can ask them to try to answer the questions *before* they read the text, using their imagination and what they already know. They can then approach the text more actively to check their answers.

- If you get students to produce questions for each other (perhaps for an **EXERCISE BOX**), you can ask them to formulate some educational questions rather than display questions.
- You can talk to teachers of other school subjects to find out what educational questions are relevant to the Theme you are working on in *CEWw*. Students can then be asked to find answers to these questions over the next week or so. You can discuss what they have found out at a specified time.
- Rather than *telling* the students, you can ask them a series of questions so that they work things out for themselves. You can ask: 'Can you think of any other similar examples?', 'Why do you think it is like that?', 'When does this happen?', 'Where?', 'Does it always happen?', 'When doesn't it happen?', 'How do you think you can find out?', 'What books would you need to look in?', 'Who could you ask?' and so on.

AtoZ READING

What and why?

Similar to **LISTENING**, **SPEAKING** and **WRITING**, there are two main roles for reading in language learning. The first is as a *goal* of learning: 'the skill of reading'. The second is as a *means* of learning: as a way of developing the students' language proficiency and educational depth. Secondary-aged students need to develop the skill of reading in English. It is through reading that they will most likely come into contact with English, particularly if they go on to higher education or are employed in international work of some kind. But reading as a *means* of learning is also important. Reading can support their language learning by contextualising and extending vocabulary, creating mental images of correct spellings, providing models for writing, and developing a 'feel' for and **MEMORY** of English.

Current theories suggest that reading is a 'psycholinguistic guessing game' in which readers constantly try to predict what is coming next in a text. While reading, readers constantly draw on what they already know about the world and the topic of the text – that is, their 'schema', to help them *bring meaning to the text*. This 'top down' approach to reading (as it is known) suggests that meaning is not simply 'in' a text – it is built up by the reader.

Reading in a second language, however, may not so easily fit into this pattern because the necessary background information and familiarity with the language may be missing – that is, the reader might not have an appropriate schema available. Second language readers, for example, may stumble on cultural references (such as place names or social customs) which first language readers take for granted. They may also have greater difficulty in deciding what they can ignore. One reason why students sometimes fail to understand a text even when they know all the vocabulary is because they cannot link what they are reading to something they already know.

Practical ideas

- Texts can also be exploited in a number of different ways:
  - Many of the texts can be used to practise re-organisation of material. For example, texts which have facts and figures can be transformed into charts or graphs; texts which report an event can be transformed into a dialogue or **ROLE PLAY**; texts which narrate an event as news can be written as a story, letter, poem or song.
  - The texts can be used to develop note-taking skills. This helps students focus on the key points of the text and to understand better how a text may be structured.
  - For **WRITING** practice, you can ask students to expand a text – they can add more to the beginning, middle and end.
  - For **VOCABULARY** practice, ask students to find the words in a text which 'go together' in a lexical set. If they have a thesaurus they can then add more words and record them in their **LANGUAGE RECORDS**.
  - Many of the texts can be used to foster **CRITICAL LANGUAGE AWARENESS**.
  - You can use the texts as a resource for discourse analysis. For example, you can ask the students to link up with a coloured pen all the references to the subject of the text. You might also ask them to identify the main ideas and any examples of each idea.
  - You can use the texts as a starting-point for **DISCUSSIONS**.
- Before asking students to read a text, you can ask them to guess what they can from the illustrations, headings and diagrams. You can also use this as an opportunity to give the students any necessary background cultural knowledge to help them establish a schema for the text.

- Many of the reading texts are also recorded on the Class Cassettes so that students can listen to the texts before, while or after they read. You can use these recordings in a variety of ways:
  - You can play part of the recording before they read the text, but ask the students to close their eyes and try to visualise the words they hear.
  - You can play the recording and ask the students to listen and make notes as they listen or afterwards. You can then discuss their notes with them before they read and check their ideas.
  - You can play the recording while students read and ask them to underline or note down all the words which do not sound the same as they are spelt (e.g. fight, countries, daughters, meant, labour).
  - You can play the recording and ask different groups of students to listen for different things – for example, names of people and places, numbers and adjectives. They can then share their ideas to reconstruct the text before they read it.
  - You can record the text yourself but make some information different or leave some information out. Students can read and find the differences.
- Students may not read very much in their mother tongue, so you may need to start by encouraging reading generally. You can do this by asking, perhaps at the start of every lesson, what they have read since the last lesson. This can be anything – a newspaper headline, a story, an advert, in the mother tongue or in English. Gradually, you can suggest that they look for things to read in English which they can tell the class about. In this way, the students can begin to see reading as something of value to share.

- As far as possible, try to create opportunities for students to read a wide range of material of their choice in English. This may vary from a library of graded readers to magazine articles chosen from boxes, comics and magazines and reference books such as encyclopaedias and textbooks in English. (Some students, for example, might enjoy reading a Maths textbook in English.) Invite (rather than require) them to tell other students (perhaps in small groups) what they have read. They don't need to report back on everything they read. The **PARCEL OF ENGLISH** scheme is a good way of exchanging a range of English language texts.
- You can allow time for silent reading in class. Some students may like to read if they finish an exercise early.
- Encourage students to read other students' writing.
- Encourage the students to guess the meaning of words they don't understand. Also, stress that they don't need to understand every word in order to read something.
- Show the students how to use a dictionary so that they can read alone.
- One common technique is to ask students to read aloud. In *CEWw*, this technique is not recommended in the classroom. Reading aloud is, in fact, a separate skill from reading for comprehension. Students are unlikely to need this skill – unless they become newsreaders! In the classroom, students typically make *more* mistakes when they read aloud than they do normally (particularly in **PRONUNCIATION**). It also wastes time for the students who have to listen, and places the teacher in the role of having to correct the reader all the time. Also, since the emphasis is on production, the main skills involved in reading – guessing words, working out meaning, predicting – are not utilised. As an 'at home' activity, however, many students may enjoy reading aloud. It can also help them to develop an image of themselves as 'an English speaker'.

A to Z ROLE PLAY

What and why?

In a role play students take on the role of another person – a waiter, an adult, even a Martian or a monster. Often the situation is given (e.g. 'You are in a restaurant. Order a meal.') and perhaps some ideas of what to say. Role play is a popular method in language-learning classrooms for a number of reasons. Students of this age find it fun and quiet students are often found to speak more openly in a 'role'. In a role play students are encouraged to use communication creatively and imaginatively and they get an opportunity to use language from 'outside' the classroom. In *CEWw*, there are role play tasks in many parts of the course, particularly in the *Out and about* sections. Role play is closely connected to **SIMULATION**.

Practical ideas

- The success of every role play depends on the students knowing exactly what they have to do. Make sure that they know the role they are going to play, some language they can use and some ideas for content.
- In general, role play works better in groups of a maximum of three or four students.
- Discuss with students how long they need to prepare their roles and whether they can prepare in pairs or alone.
- Students can prepare either in 'complete' groups for the role play (that is, one student for each character) or in character groups (that is, in small groups they share ideas of what they will each say, and then join with other students when they are ready to act out the role play).

- Some students like to make notes of what they are going to say. This creates confidence in the preparation period, but you should encourage students to speak without reading out their notes.
- As a role play is based on 'real-life situations', if you have some 'realia' (real items) from an English-speaking country (e.g. real menus, real bus/train timetables, real/plastic English/American/Australian money, etc.), these will make the role play more fun. Younger students often like to have 'props' – handbags, shopping bags, purses, etc.
- During the preparation stage the role of the teacher is to circulate, answering questions, checking that everyone understands, and making suggestions.
- You may need to remind students of some 'checking' and 'communication' phrases: 'Sorry? Could you say that again please?', 'What do you mean?', 'What's the word for …?'.
- During the role play itself you can listen and write notes about points which can be discussed later. If a student gets stuck, indicate to the others to help in any way they

can. You can prepare a comments sheet like the one below. The students who are listening to the role play can also make a note of their comments.

Name:

Language areas	To comment on	To praise
Grammar		
Vocabulary		
Pronunciation		
Communication		
Self-correction		
General comments		

- After the role play discuss with the class how they felt it went and then put general points on the board to avoid embarrassing individual students.
- Sometimes it is a good idea to record the role play on audio or video cassette so that you and the students can see/hear it again later.

AtoZ SIMULATION

What and why?

Simulation is very closely related to the concept of **ROLE PLAY**. The main difference is that in a role play students are usually told *who* they are and *what* they have to say. For example, one student might be a waiter in a restaurant and the other might be a customer – their roles are clearly defined, they both know what will happen, and what they are expected to say. A simulation is much more **OPEN-ENDED**. Students are placed in a situation where they will have to make decisions. Normally, they can still be themselves and they can contribute the knowledge and experience they have from the outside world. The outcomes of a simulation can therefore be different every time the simulation is done.

Simulations are very useful for developing the students' **FLUENCY**. They give the students the experience of working with language that is less controlled and to develop the skills necessary for using English outside the classroom.

Practical ideas

- The key to a successful simulation is to ensure that everyone understands exactly what they are expected to do and what situation they are in.
- It is normally best to avoid **ERROR CORRECTION** during the simulation, as this will interrupt the flow of the conversation and thought. See **ROLE PLAY**.
- Before a simulation begins, it is usually a good idea to make sure that students know exactly how much time they have got.
- After a simulation, you can spend some time discussing why they came to the decisions that they did, and whether all members of the group were happy with the decisions.
- Students could record their simulation on audio or video cassette.

AtoZ SKIMMING AND SCANNING

What and why?

Skimming and scanning are two different **READING** skills. Skimming means looking at a text or chapter quickly in order to have a general idea of the contents. Scanning means looking at a text to find some particular information. For example, we skim through a report to have a rough idea of what it says but we scan a page of the telephone directory to find a particular name or number. Skimming requires a greater degree of reading and word recognition skills as it involves a more thorough understanding of the text. Scanning to find a

particular piece of information can be achieved successfully by relatively poor readers and is therefore a very satisfying achievement for those daunted by texts in a foreign language. As the students become more confident of their reading ability in the mother tongue and in English, they will learn how to approach texts with different reading skills depending on the purpose of the text and the purpose they have for reading it. The more students are encouraged to approach a text by first using skimming or scanning techniques, the sooner they begin to realise that they do not have to read and understand every word of a text. Slow readers are 'text-bounded', that is, they think that they have to work laboriously through every word in order to understand a text.

Practical ideas

- Both skimming and scanning are practised in many exercises in the *Topic* and *Language* Units.
- Use scanning techniques at the beginning of the year to familiarise students with the Student's Book. The task can be a race between four teams in the class. For example, with *CEWw 1* you could ask them to turn to the *Wordlist/Index* and to find the word which is after 'airport'. The first person to find it gets a point for the team. Then ask them to find a word which is above 'film', then three below another word and on the same line in another column. Then ask them to look at the map at the beginning of the book and to find a Unit about 'Poems', for example, or other titles of Themes or Units.

- It is useful to explain the difference between skimming and scanning to the students (give them the example of a telephone directory and a chapter of a History/Science textbook).
- Before the students read a text, ask them whether they think the task requires them to skim or to scan the text.
- Students often like having races. Occasionally ask students to see who can find the information in a text first.
- Allow time for students to read the texts quietly to themselves in class to practise their own technique. Texts do not need to be read out loud round the class.
- Encourage students to practise skimming and scanning when they read in their mother tongue.
- Students can write 'skim' and 'scan' questions for other students at the beginning of each Theme or *Topic* and *Language* Unit.

AtoZ SPEAKING

What and why?

One of the main aims of *CEWw* is to give students confidence in expressing themselves orally. The emphasis is, therefore, on spoken fluency rather than on spoken accuracy. This should encourage students to be confident and creative in their spoken English.

Practical ideas

- Before correcting a spoken error, consider whether it could lead to misunderstanding. If not, there may be little reason to correct it. Too much **ERROR CORRECTION** can inhibit the students' desire to speak.
- Encourage students to give their reactions to the pictures and input at the start of a Unit. There is no need to insist on whole sentences – they may only manage a phrase or even a word. Try to react to *what* they have said rather than *how* they have said it.
- Allow space and time for the students to speak! You can record some of your lessons and calculate how much time *you* spend talking and how much time *the students* spend talking. If necessary, see if you can change the situation over the term.

- Students often find it difficult to provide a rapid spoken reply to a question without time to **PROCESS** an answer. Sometimes it may be useful to give the students the questions you will ask them in advance so they can prepare. At the beginning, it may be better to let students volunteer a reply rather than insist that they answer in turn.
- The quieter students may prefer to be given the choice of speaking on to a cassette at home. They could then, perhaps, give you the cassette to listen to.
- Try to ensure that different people speak each time. You can suggest that different people do the reporting back after **GROUPWORK**.
- If you have some students who never say anything, or who **PARTICIPATE** very little, you need to ask yourself why this is. It may be their preferred **LEARNING STRATEGY**/style (to listen and absorb), they may feel shy, they may feel that they don't know enough, or they may feel that the lessons are dominated by other students. If the situation persists, you could talk to the students concerned to find out what they think about it. It may not be a problem for them at all!

AtoZ SPELLING

What and why?

Many students – and many native English speakers – find English spelling difficult. Since English has been influenced by many other languages, it does not have a completely consistent 'fit' between the way it is spoken and the way it is written. In addition, the invention of printing in the 15th century had the effect of 'fixing' the spelling of English at a

time when the language was undergoing many changes.

'Good spelling' is important. It influences the way people think of you, and your ability to communicate clearly. However, it is important not to over-emphasise spelling. For many students, spelling is something that takes care of itself as they get more exposure to English. In the initial stages of learning, a stress on correct spelling may discourage students from using the language to try to express what they want to express. Some students may have problems in spelling in their own language, and drawing attention to this in English may strengthen their feeling of failure. The best approach is probably to point out spellings to students, and to do a little practice frequently.

Practical ideas

- Ensure that the students understand that sometimes there is little or no relationship between pronunciation and spelling in English. You can make this fun by saying, for example, 'We say two /tuː/ but we write /twəʊ/.' You get them to count in 'spelling English': /əʊneɪ/, /twəʊ/, /t h reɪ/ and so on.
- If all your students share the same **MOTHER TONGUE** it is likely that they make the same spelling errors. Make a list of them and, if possible, put the correct version on a **POSTER** on the wall. Students can then refer to this when they are writing.
- You could give the students groups of words to learn, grouped around sounds. For example, /iː/ words: 'sweet', 'feet', 'meat', 'heat', etc. Point out to students how the same sound is spelt in different ways.
- Do the spelling errors fall into groups? For example, perhaps students have trouble remembering the double consonant in some comparatives and superlatives, or perhaps they confuse 'ei' with 'ie'. With the students, you could draw up a checklist of their common errors. They can then use this checklist every time they write something.
- Encourage the students to check spellings in the *Wordlist/Index* at the back of their Student's Book.
- 'Good spelling' probably comes with **READING**. The more the students read, the more it is likely to help their spelling. After the students have read a text, you could ask them to go back and focus on the words. Ask them to write down (or underline/circle) any words which they think they will have trouble spelling correctly later. Discuss with the group their choices and find out why they chose those words.

- To encourage students to look closely at common letter patterns, after they have read a text, write some two-, three- or four-letter patterns on the board (for example, 'ea', 'ough', 'th'). Then ask them, individually or in teams, to find as many examples as possible of those letter patterns in the text.
- Students can test each other in groups.
- Play 'Spelling Snap!' in groups of three or four. On one side of some cards, write words which students know but may find difficult. Make sure there are at least three examples of each of the letter patterns. Shuffle the cards. Each student has 10 or so cards. Students take it in turns to put one of their cards in the centre of the table and say the word on the card at the same time. If the card which follows has the same letter pattern they must shout 'Snap!'. The person with the most cards at the end is the winner.

Researching the classroom

- To find out if students who have problems with spelling in English also have problems in **MOTHER TONGUE** spelling, ask their other subject teachers if you can see some of their work. Alternatively, you can dictate a short text in the mother tongue to the students (perhaps about a *CES* Theme). Collect in the papers and make a note of the errors and the students who made them. Give another brief dictation in English and compare the results.
- To find out the nature of spelling problems that your students have, make a list of the words that they misspell when you correct their work. After a few weeks, see if you can put the words into groups. Are there particular sounds that they consistently misspell? Are there words that they confuse? (e.g. *right* and *write*)
- Does pressure of time affect the students' spelling? Give them a short period of time and ask them to write as much as they can about a topic. Some time later, suggest another topic and divide the time up: 15 minutes to write, five minutes to check and change. Compare the results.
- Are your students aware of their spelling difficulties? When they write something, ask them to underline the words they are not sure how to spell. Compare this with the mistakes they make.

A to Z STUDENT INVOLVEMENT

What and why?

Student involvement is probably the single most important factor in language learning, especially with students in the early secondary school years. One of the greatest causes of drop-out and student failure in learning is that they do not feel part of their course. For this reason, the encouragement of student involvement is one of the key principles in *CEWw*. The aim is to involve the students as fully as possible in their English course, so that they feel it is *theirs* and personally relevant to them. *CEWw* contains numerous practical ideas

in relation to student involvement. The following are some of the basic principles we have adopted.

Practical ideas

- Start from the students. When introducing a new topic, find out what the students already know about it and what they would like to know about it.
- Encourage regular **EVALUATION** of how they are learning and take steps accordingly.

- Provide choices between tasks. Students do not have to be doing the same things all the time. Allow them to **DECIDE** and make room for **DO IT YOURSELF**.
- Provide creative tasks which draw on the students' imagination, experience and personal views.
- Provide 'larger' **TASKS**, such as whole activities, where students can feel freer to work in their own way.

- Draw on the **MOTHER TONGUE** as a means of involving the students' knowledge about how language works.
- Involve students in the production of **TESTS** and make tests less threatening.
- Focus on topics which are worth learning about in their own right, and which have **CURRICULUM LINKS**.

AtoZ STUDENT TEST-WRITING

What and why?

In all levels of *CEWw*, students can become involved in writing their own tests. Student-designed tests are not intended to replace the tests that you or the school might set – there will always be a need for external tests of some kind. Most tests, however, give students very little – student test-writing is a way of making tests a *learning* device as well as a testing one. Students can learn a lot from making their own tests for a number of reasons. Firstly, it requires them to do some investigation, to focus carefully on a structure or meaning and to use it. Secondly, it helps to break down the fear of tests which many students have and allows them to see tests as an opportunity to find out how much they know. Thirdly, it helps to integrate the class as it provides a means for students to challenge each other.

Practical ideas

- If your students are new to the idea of writing tests, it is a good idea to get them to do a simple test first and then to look at the way it is designed.
- Before students work on making their own tests, you can first ask the class what they have learned in recent lessons. You can build up a list of their suggestions on the board. This will also give you an idea of how much they remember.
- Students can work in groups to produce test sections on different areas of language – for example, one group can work on a grammar area, another on the vocabulary, and so on; or groups can produce different kinds of tests on the same language area – for example, to test vocabulary one group can write a dialogue with questions, another group can make a puzzle, another can make a gap-fill exercise, and so on.
- The students can exchange tests with other classes or include them in a **PARCEL OF ENGLISH**.
- Tests they have already done can be placed in an **EXERCISE BOX**.

AtoZ TASKS

What and why?

The word 'task' is used in a variety of meanings in language teaching. One common use is in the sense of 'whole tasks', that is, a large classroom activity in which the students may be doing a variety of different things. In this sense, the optional *Activity* Units are 'whole tasks'. The focus in 'whole task' work is usually on meaning rather than the form of the language, although both are important (see **FLUENCY**). Many writers argue that teaching through 'whole tasks' is most effective since students can learn the language through natural processes of acquisition.

In *CEWw*, however, the word 'task' is used in the same way as 'exercise', to refer to any structured language-learning procedure. 'Task' in this sense will include everything from a gap-fill exercise to a poetry-writing activity. Tasks may be 'small' and may only take a few minutes (such as doing a word puzzle) or they may be 'large' and take a whole lesson or more (such as making a poster). In actual fact, 'large tasks' are likely to be made up of smaller tasks. Some of the key questions in language teaching are: 'What are the most effective kinds of tasks for language learning?', 'What makes a

task more or less difficult for students?', 'How do different kinds of tasks affect classroom interaction?', 'How do different kinds of tasks shape **LEARNING STRATEGIES**?' and 'What roles do different kinds of tasks place on teachers and students?'

Practical ideas

- See the *A to Z* entries on **TASKS IN BLOCKS**, **OPEN-ENDED TASKS**, **AUTONOMY**, **CRITICAL PEDAGOGY**, **EXERCISE BOX**, **DECIDE ... EXERCISES**, **DO IT YOURSELF**, **PROBLEM SOLVING**, **MIXED ABILITIES**, **FLUENCY** and other cross-references.

Researching the classroom

- Experiment with different ways of doing similar tasks to see if that affects student performance. For example, writing can be done individually or in small groups, with or without planning and **BRAINSTORMING**, or with or without dictionary support, and so on.
- Choose two or three tasks which seem to be very different in nature. For example, a poster-making activity, a grammar discovery task and a reading comprehension task. Then choose three or four students in your class. When you come to those tasks in

your teaching, watch how the students respond individually to different kinds of tasks. Do some students prefer to work in a particular way? Do they seem to achieve more from particular kinds of tasks?

- Give a lot of support initially in a particular area and then gradually reduce that support to see when it becomes difficult for the students. For example, if the students are doing listening work, you can initially teach them the language they will hear, give them an overview in their own language, let them listen with their books open, and then listen several times. Gradually reduce the support (for example, they can listen with their books closed) to see at what point it becomes difficult for them. You can then discover how much support you actually need to give.

- Do the tasks that the students do in your lessons emphasise particular **LEARNING STRATEGIES** and classroom roles? When you are planning a lesson, sometimes look back over your plan and analyse the main tasks with the following questions: 1 What role will the students take? Will they be initiating language or responding? 2 What mental process will they have to go through? (E.g. repeating, analysing, planning, recalling from memory.) 3 What is the task about? Where does most of the subject matter come from? From the book, from the students, from the teacher? If you continually get the same answers to these questions, try to identify ways in which you can change the focus of your lesson to create greater variety and learning opportunities.

A to Z TASKS IN BLOCKS

What and why?

A situation which often arises in teaching is that some students, working either in groups or alone, finish before others. This may not be a problem. There is no particular reason, for example, why students should have to be kept 100% busy 100% of the time. In some cases, however, students may waste their time as they wait for others to catch up. This may lead to boredom, disenchantment with learning English and, in some cases, **DISCIPLINE** problems. Putting tasks in blocks is a technique which ensures that students have something to go on to when they finish their work.

Practical ideas

- Before students start working, you can put two or three tasks together 'in a block'. Go through the tasks, explaining what the students have to do in each one. As they finish one task, they can move on to the next.
- You can put some tasks in blocks with the **TIME TO SPARE?** sections and an **EXERCISE BOX**, if you are using one. Students will then have something to do when they finish the tasks.
- Putting tasks in blocks will give you more time for **MONITORING AND GUIDING**.
- You can give a time limit for the tasks. If they finish before, students can move on to anything else they wish, providing it is related to learning English (see **TIME TO SPARE?** and **EXERCISE BOX**).

TEACHING ADOLESCENTS

What and why?

Teachers' views on the teaching of adolescents vary enormously. Some love it, and would not choose to teach any other age range. Probably almost as many, however, find it difficult, often more difficult the older the adolescent students become. The first important point to make, however, is that it is difficult, if not impossible, to generalise about 'adolescence'. There is enormous variation in the nature of the adolescent period from individual to individual, and from culture to culture. In some cultures, children seem to remain 'children' longer; in others they appear to grow up very quickly. Some adolescents find the movement from being 'a child' to being 'an adult' a very troublesome one, whilst others do not experience any particular problems. What is clear is that during the period of adolescence, an individual's sense of *who they are* may often go through many transformations. Bodily changes as well as rapid changes in opinions, tastes, habits and relations between the sexes may combine to give the impression that it is not one person that we are dealing with, but several!

Parents and teachers of adolescents often report that the period can place great strain on their relationships. Adolescents may be seeking independence and this may conflict with the views of the parents/teachers. As the time may be a period of great change for the adolescent, they may often seem restless – unsure if they are doing what they want to do or should be doing. They may also be anxious about the future: 'What is to become of me?', 'What next?', 'Will I cope?', 'What will happen if ...?' All of these things may require great patience from everyone concerned.

Practical ideas

Given that the period of adolescence is so changeable, it is difficult to offer clear advice about how to best handle the teaching of adolescents. There are, however, some general points which teachers have shared with us and which we have found useful.

- Be patient. Things may take longer to achieve in the classroom than you anticipate. The students may seem tired or unwilling. Very often this is because of factors completely outside the classroom.

- Be flexible. Conflicts can be avoided if the teacher is prepared to be flexible about when and how things are done. This may be a matter of tolerating classroom behaviour that you don't approve of, for example. However, you have to also make clear the limits of what you are prepared to accept.
- Be sensitive. Teachers often report that adolescent students are frequently moody – they can be happy and bright one day and deflated the next day. As a teacher, it is important for you to keep note of these changes and, where necessary, talk to the student to see if they are having problems.
- Allow choice and student decisions. It may also be useful if you can be flexible about what the students do.

If you can provide them with choice and allow room for their personal interests, you are likely to find it much easier working with them. You can also involve them in decisions about what you will do in the lessons and ask them to plan activities, choose texts, music and so on.

- Show respect. The students must have a clear sense of respect for you as the teacher, but equally you must have a sense of respect for them – recognising, for example, that their opinions, tastes in clothes, music, etc. are equally valid. That said, your role is as an educator, so it should remain your responsibility to encourage students to question what they are saying or doing, and to ensure that limits are set and maintained for the benefit of everyone.
- See also **STUDENT INVOLVEMENT**, **DISCIPLINE** and **DECIDE … EXERCISES**.

AtoZ TESTS

What and why?

Tests can form a useful and important role in language learning. They can give both the students and the teacher a clear picture of how much the students have learnt. They can also give the students a focus on something to work towards, and thus motivation for learning. However, tests can also have many negative consequences. Some students can become very anxious about tests and this can prevent them from effective learning. Students may become so focused on the test that they lose sight of the wider goal – learning English. Learning can also become 'defensive', in that they learn something because of the fear of the test but rapidly forget it once the test has passed. For these reasons, tests need to be handled carefully and made more 'friendly' to the students.

Practical ideas

- Before a test, give the students a clear list of what they will be tested on. They can then be asked to rate themselves on each area of the test and compare with the marks after the test.
- Try to view a test not so much as an indication of how much the students know/don't know but as an indication of how effective classroom language teaching is. If students perform badly, this may say more about what is happening/not happening in the classroom than it does about the students.
- In all levels of *CEWw*, students can be involved in devising their own tests (see **STUDENT TEST-WRITING**). Students can learn from the process of writing the test and seeing their own corrected version. The test is then also 'theirs' rather than 'yours', and so less threatening.
- Students can be given practice tests to do at home. These give the students the opportunity to test themselves without anxiety.

AtoZ TIME TO SPARE?

What and why?

Students work at a different **PACE** and some finish exercises more quickly or slowly than others. The *Time to spare?* sections (at the end of the *Topic* and *Language* Units) are designed to give students something to go on with if they finish ahead of the others.

Practical ideas

- The *Time to spare?* sections contain extra exercises and the option of creating an exercise (which could be put into a class **EXERCISE BOX**). Students might also want to choose a **DO IT YOURSELF** task.

- Students don't need to be kept 100% busy 100% of the time. If they do finish early, they can be given the option of just relaxing, as long as they don't disturb other students. Getting more work as a reward for working hard can be very demotivating!
- The photocopiable *Language worksheets* at the back of the Teacher's Book might also be given to students if they have time to spare.

AtoZ TIMING

What and why?

The timing and PACE of each lesson are linked together. However, timing refers mainly to *when* things are done in the lesson. The rhythm of the lesson needs to be maintained so that students use the class time productively and enjoyably. Your timing for new activities or steps in the lesson also needs to bear in mind what the students have just been doing and how much time is left in the lesson.

Practical ideas

- Look at the timing estimates in the teaching notes for each Unit before you start and write your own estimates.
- Make a note during the lesson of the actual time each exercise took with each class and, if appropriate, why you think it differed from your estimates.
- Before starting an exercise, tell the students how long they have. Near the end of the time, warn them that the time is almost over.
- Keep an eye on the clock during the lesson: don't start a new task just before the end of the lesson!
- If there are only a few minutes left at the end of the lesson, the students can work on the TIME TO SPARE? exercises, fill in their LANGUAGE RECORD, do an exercise from the EXERCISE BOX, make an exercise, play a game, sing a song, or look back through the previous Units.

AtoZ TRANSLATION

What and why?

As a technique in language learning and teaching, translation used to be very popular. In recent years, however, it has fallen out of favour. There has been concern that an over-use of translation encourages the students to produce very strange-sounding English. Too much translation can also prevent students from developing fluency in the language as they develop the habit of going through their MOTHER TONGUE. Yet, used appropriately, there are a number of reasons why translation, as a teaching technique, still offers considerable benefits. Students, at all levels of ability, *do* translate. It is, in fact, impossible to learn anything unless you find ways of integrating it into what you already know – in this case the mother tongue. It is thus important that the teacher is able to ensure that students have the *correct* translation in their minds. Translation can also help students be themselves – they can express what they want to say and then learn how to say those same things in English. It is also useful as a planning device (e.g. before writing) where trying to plan in English would prevent the flow of ideas.

Practical ideas

- You can deal with basic vocabulary problems through translation. This saves time compared with long explanations and ensures the correct meaning is understood.
- Students can play the translation game, where a 'non-English-speaking' student says something in the mother tongue and another student has to interpret for him/her.
- BRAINSTORMING can be done in the mother tongue, but as you put the ideas up on the board or a POSTER, you can translate them into English. Students can then learn from seeing *their* ideas in English.
- Before doing a ROLE PLAY, WRITING a passage, preparing QUESTIONS or an exercise, students can first plan things out in their mother tongue, all the time thinking of what they are able to say in English. Planning in the mother tongue can prevent language problems interfering with the generating of ideas.

AtoZ VIDEO

What and why?

In general, students find the use of videos motivating and stimulating. Videos are a useful vehicle for learning more about a topic, for making cross-cultural comparisons and for making the language more memorable. *CEWw* is accompanied by a set of videos. These can be used together with the coursebooks or on their own. The videos are not intended simply to provide 'language models'. They aim to enrich the students' knowledge and experience of language use in relation to the topics in the course by providing interesting extension material for each of the six Themes at each level of the course. See the video packs themselves for further details of the videos and accompanying worksheets. The following notes apply to the use of videos in general. (There are also further general ideas with the video booklets.)

Practical ideas

- Plan ahead! Book the video player and the video cassette. Check if a technician will be available. Watch the video and read through the video script before the lesson so that you are aware of the language, characters, topic and content.
- Prepare the students before they see the video so that they have an idea of what they are going to see. Give them a general outline of what they will see. This will make it much easier for them to follow and learn.
- You can set some tasks before the students watch the video. These can be of a general nature, about what happens in the video. After the students have watched the extract from the video all the way through, you can follow this up with further detailed tasks which require the students to listen or look for detail.
- Tip: When you start the cassette put the counter on zero so that when you rewind and replay you will find the place more easily.
- Tip: Make sure that all the students can see the screen and hear.
- Keep the video session fairly short. Ten minutes of video every week is more useful than 40 minutes every month.

Some ideas for exploiting videos:
- Play the video the first time without any sound. Ask the students what they think the people are saying.
- Students can watch the section all the way through. Rewind, then play a part again. Then freeze the frame and ask them if they can remember what comes next.
- Observation: the students can do this in teams. Give them a list of items before the viewing. They have to write down who had or did them, e.g. 'Who had a red car?', 'Who had glasses?', 'Who did Peter talk to?', etc.
- After viewing the video extract once, students can work in groups to write questions for each other. They can then exchange these and watch the video again to find the answers.
- Talk about cross-cultural aspects. Ask students to write down after the viewing four things they noticed which were different from their culture (objects, buildings, clothes, food, etc.) and four things which were the same. Put them on the board. Discuss why the things are the same or different.
- In advance, choose some sentences from the video script and ask students what they think the video will be about, what they will learn about and so on. They can also guess who says the sentences, why, etc.
- Students can also be involved in making their own videos.

AtoZ VOCABULARY

What and why?

Vocabulary is possibly the single most important area in language learning. With a large vocabulary, a person can communicate effectively even though he/she may be very weak in grammatical knowledge. In *CEWw*, vocabulary development is thus emphasised. This is achieved through various vocabulary-related exercises, the students' **LANGUAGE RECORDS** and the **HELP YOURSELF LIST** (or *Ideas list*) in the Student's Book, and the *Vocabulary maps* (from *CEWw 3* onwards). It can be expected, however, that the students' *passive* knowledge of vocabulary (their understanding) will always be greater than their *active* abilities (what they are able to produce). The same is likely to be true in the mother tongue.

Practical ideas

- Writing vocabulary puzzles for an **EXERCISE BOX**, for a **PARCEL OF ENGLISH** or for their partner gives students time to absorb new words.
- Encourage students to compare new words with translations in the **MOTHER TONGUE**.
- Encourage students to guess new words in texts.
- Show the students how they can use a dictionary. This will help them build up their vocabulary outside of class time.

- Students can be put into small groups to test each other on vocabulary or to devise a vocabulary test for the class.
- For each Theme, the students could gradually construct a large vocabulary puzzle. Decide in advance with the students what kind you will make – for example, a word search (with words hidden in a square of letters), an acrostic (where words run down through one long word), a traditional crossword puzzle or a circular puzzle (where the last letter of one word is the first letter of the next) – and put the plan on the wall. During the two or three weeks of the Theme each student puts a clue on the puzzle. At the end of the Theme, students write the clues and the blank puzzle in their books and do the puzzle together.
- 'I spy' is a lively vocabulary game which younger students like playing. One student says 'I spy with my little eye something beginning with "w".' The object must be in the room. Students guess. The one to get it right has the next turn.

Researching the classroom

Most research suggests that it is far easier to learn vocabulary in 'chunks' of meaning than as isolated words. This is one of the main reasons why *CES* is designed around Themes. This gives a context with which the students can associate language and thus makes it more memorable. You can see the effect of context, meaning and association with a few simple experiments with one of your classes.

- Give your students a list of 20 random words to learn and, at the same time, a short passage about something interesting. Test their ability to recall it in **WRITING**. Ask them to write down *anything* they remember from the list and *anything* from the passage (for the purposes of this experiment, ignore **SPELLING** mistakes). One week and two weeks later, test the students on both things again. Which do they remember most? How much is lost from the list and from the passage?

- Try a similar experiment but, this time, actively involve the students with the language in some way in order to build up associations with the language. For example, you could identify each word on the list with a part of the room (ask the students to imagine that the word 'street' is in the corner of the room, 'traffic' is near the window, 'airport' is near the door and so on). A week later, point to each part of the room and see if they can recall the word.
- You can try a similar experiment with remembering 'chunks' of text. Ask the students to act it out, perhaps in pairs as a dialogue. Or perhaps they could sing it or associate physical movement with each sentence.

AtoZ WRITING

What and why?

In common with **LISTENING**, **READING** and **SPEAKING**, there are two main roles for writing in language teaching. The first is as a *goal* of learning. It is important for students to develop the writing skill in order to express themselves in written English in letters, messages, stories, and so on. The second role, however, is as a *means* of learning. Writing can provide further sources of practice and can help the students remember the words, phrases, grammar, etc. that they are learning. By working on writing tasks, students can become closely involved with the language and, in doing so, develop their general language proficiency. Writing can thus form a very important element in the course.

Practical ideas

- Encourage the students to keep written records of what they learn. The **LANGUAGE RECORD** will be useful in this respect.
- Before calling on the students to do any large oral activity, such as **ROLE PLAY**, students can be encouraged to plan in writing what they are going to say.
- Where students are involved in writing as a *goal* of language learning, encourage them to go through the various stages of collecting ideas, drafting, getting

FEEDBACK from a reader, revising and final production. You can incorporate these stages of development into a **PROCESS WRITING** approach.
- Where possible, give the students real-life tasks which have a real audience. This could be writing a letter requesting information, making a **PARCEL OF ENGLISH**, writing to pen-friends and so on. Writing to other students can also provide an audience (see **INTERACTIVE WRITING**).
- In correcting students' writing, try not to over-correct. A page full of red ink can be very demoralising! There are a number of alternative ways of approaching **ERROR CORRECTION**:
  - Ask the students to underline the things they are not sure of or where they would like your help – you need only then correct the things they have identified.
  - Limit yourself to no more than six to eight points for correction.
  - Rather than focusing on the form of what they have written, respond to the message. Write a brief reply to the ideas they have expressed.
  - Rather than correcting, give hints or clues and encourage the students to correct their own work. You can use a marking scheme (e.g. Sp = spelling, WW = wrong word, and so on).

ZERO LEVEL

What and why?

'Zero level' is the term often used to refer to students who are at the very beginning of learning a language, or at the beginning of learning a particular aspect of language (such as the Past tense). The term 'zero level', however, suggests that they come to us knowing nothing, and this may have an impact on *how* we teach them. If we assume they know nothing, then we may see our task as getting language 'into their heads' – filling 'the empty bucket' as the philosopher Karl Popper, once described it. This can place students into a passive role in the classroom, where they are to simply 'learn what they are taught'. In actual fact, all students come to the classroom knowing a lot – about the world, about their experiences, about how language is used – and, particularly in the case of younger students, full of imagination and ideas. It may be true that they know little of the foreign language – although they probably know more than we think – but if we emphasise the foreign language aspect (rather than their ideas and experiences), then we will limit their possibilities of contributing to the classroom.

Practical ideas

- In *CEWw*, the initial emphasis in each Unit is on the topic or content. Language is presented as a way of communicating ideas, not just as 'grammar'. When the emphasis is on a topic, there is more possibility for the students to contribute what they have learnt elsewhere. In these initial stages, the accuracy of their language is not so important. The vital thing is that there is the possibility for them to understand and exchange ideas.
- When students are sharing ideas/information about a topic, you can help them to say what they want to say in English. Provide key phrases and words *as they need them*. This way, they will relate to the new language as their language.
- **BRAINSTORMING** is an excellent way of finding out what students know about something before you begin.
- If you are teaching a new language area, you can ask the students how they express those ideas in their mother tongue. For example, if you are teaching the function of asking for information, you might ask them how they would ask different people for the loan of a pen – a friend, a very small child, a stranger in the street, a teacher and so on. This way, they can see that they naturally have the ability to adjust their language to different situations. You can do the same with areas of grammar, particularly where English is different from the mother tongue.
- It is often useful to ask students to do an **OPEN-ENDED TASK** before you teach a new language area. Choose a task which naturally uses the language that you intend to teach. For example, if you are about to teach the Past simple, you might ask the students to brainstorm what they know about the life of cavepeople. Often we are surprised by what they can produce.
- You can also ask students to share ideas about an area of grammar before you teach it. For example, you could ask them, in pairs, to note down *any* words they know for talking about the past in English. You could put some ideas on the board in the mother tongue (e.g. 'yesterday', 'last night', '100 years ago', 'I was').

Four articles on language teaching

Andrew Littlejohn describes some ways that teachers can identify a 'good task' and make good tasks even better.

The importance of 'tasks'

In most English language classes, the amount of time that teachers and students spend communicating *directly* with each other is usually quite low. Most of what teachers and students say to each other is shaped, instead, by the tasks that they are doing. We can say, then, that tasks are an 'interface' between teachers and students – it is *through* a task that they communicate with each other. Tasks are important, then, in determining the *rights* that students have and what they are permitted to say. This means that it is very important to look closely at what tasks ask teachers and students to do. To help us do this, we can compare two very different types of tasks. The first type of task is, I am sure, a familiar one. The second type, perhaps less so.

Two examples of tasks

Task 1: A visit to the museum

For this first type of task, imagine that the students have just been learning Present simple question forms. The teacher now divides the students into pairs. One student in each pair is A and the other B. Each student is then given a role card.

Student A

You want to go to the museum. You want to know the following:
– what time the museum opens
– what time it closes
– how much a ticket costs
– if there is a restaurant
You ring the museum to find out.

Student B

You work at the museum. Here is some information.

CITY MUSEUM
Admission: £2.00; Children free
Open: 10.30 – 5.30 Mon – Sat;
10.30 – 12.30 Sunday.
The restaurant closes 30 minutes later.

Does it look familiar? In the modern day 'communicative' classroom, this is probably one of the most common types of task: 'the information gap'. Students begin working in pairs, getting plenty of practice in asking and answering questions guided by their role cards. To this extent, the task is very successful. Or is it? Before we discuss this question, let's look at a very different type of task.

Task 2: A question poster

Imagine that another class, all young learners, has just been working on a page in their coursebook about animals. They have learned the names of some animals, talked briefly about what they can see, and then listened to some sounds on the cassette, where they have to guess which animal makes that sound.

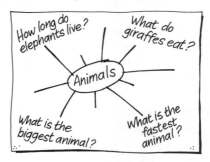

From *Cambridge English for the World, Teacher's Book 1*

The teacher then sticks a large piece of paper on the wall, writes 'Animal World' in the centre, and draws a circle around it with a question on a line: 'What do giraffes eat?'. The teacher then says to the class:

'Look at the pictures in your book. What questions do YOU have about the animals?'

Students then begin suggesting questions. Initially, many of these come in the mother tongue, but as the teacher writes them up, the students start suggesting their own questions in English. The teacher points to the use of 'do' and 'can' in the questions on the board, and encourages the students to form their own questions in a similar way. When quite a few questions are on the board, the teacher says:

'Look at these questions. I want you to try to find the answers. Ask your friends, look in books, ask your parents and teachers – see what you can find out. At the end of our next lessons, we can spend 10 minutes seeing what answers you have found.'

Over the next few lessons, the teacher asks the students what answers they have. The teacher writes these answers in simple English on a piece of paper and sticks them next to the question on the question poster.

Different roles for teachers and learners

As you can see, the tasks are very different. How would you answer these questions about each task?

- What is the aim of the task?
- Where do the ideas and language come from?
- How personally involving is the task?
- What happens to what the students produce?

You might like to think about your answers before you read my own.

Task 1: A visit to the museum

There is no doubt that information gap tasks such as the 'museum' example are often very useful. They provide good opportunities for language work. They do have some important limitations, however. The main aim of the task is purely a language one: to provide practise in question forms. For this reason, if the students are already proficient in using question forms, *the task will have little or no value*.

The task is also tightly structured and all of the ideas in it are provided by the role cards. The language, too, mainly comes directly from the role cards – students simply have to apply a grammar rule. Once the task is over, the details of it can be forgotten – its sole purpose is to practise grammar. It would be very unlikely, for example, for the teacher to begin the next lesson with the question 'What time does the museum open?' The level of personal involvement is therefore quite low. In fact, if you were to do the task with different classes, even in different countries, the result would be almost identical in each case. We can say, then, that the task produces a 'standardised classroom'.

Task 2: A question poster

If we use the same four questions to think about the question poster task, we get a very different set of answers. We can see immediately that the aim of the task goes far beyond language learning. While the students get exposure to and practice in using question forms (as in Task 1) they are also developing wider *educational* abilities: drawing on their own knowledge, formulating genuine questions, and researching. The task therefore *will continue to have value even if students are already proficient in question forms*. They are also more personally involved in what is going on – the questions all come from them. This places the teacher in a different role. In the museum task, we can say that the teacher's role is mainly what I call 'the language policeman' – checking that the students are producing language correctly. In the question poster task, however, the teacher's role changes to one of supporting the students, helping them to say *what they want to say*. This means, then, that every time a class does the task, the outcome will be different: the task produces a 'unique classroom', shaped by the unique individuals who are in it.

Making good tasks better: 'dimensions of tasks'

Looking closely at the museum task and the question poster task, we can see some important differences. We can draw these together as 'dimensions' of tasks which will help us to see what a task offers – and how we can improve it.

Value beyond language learning

The first dimension measures the value that a task has in addition to language learning. At one end, we can place 'language specific goals' – that is, the students will only be learning language – such that if they are already proficient in the language area of the task, then *the task will have no value*. At the other end, we can place a much broader value: 'wider educational goals', which will mean that even if the students are proficient in the language area, *the task will still have value*. Tasks might fall anyway between these two points.

Value beyond language learning	
Language specific goals	Wider educational goals

Looking at tasks in this way, we can see that we can improve a task if we can give it educational value. We might do this, for example, by using more educational content – instead of a fictional museum, for example, students might be asking about important real places.

The role of the learner

One of the most striking things about the museum task, is that the students hardly have to think – everything is supplied by the task. In contrast, the question poster task asks the students to supply almost everything. This suggests another way to analyse tasks.

The role of the learner	
Consumer ideas and language supplied by the task	Producer ideas and language supplied by the learners

Again, we can see that we could improve a task if we increase the amount of ideas and language that the students are expected to produce. In the museum task, for example, instead of giving the students everything, we might ask them what questions they would ask and ask them to invent the information.

Free and controlled work

My final two dimensions look more closely at the design of a task. Every task has two elements: *what*, that is, the topic (e.g. museums, animals, etc.) and *how* (e.g. information gap in pairs). For each element, we can see how much 'freedom' or 'control' there is for the student. We can then we put these two elements next to each other, and build a graph, like this:

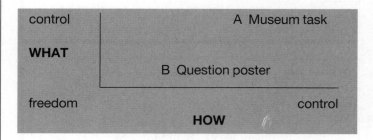

Thinking about the museum task, for example, we can see that there is a lot of control over *what* the students say and *how* they work. On the graph, we can probably put it at point A. The question poster task, however, is rather different. There is still some control over what they say and some control over how they produce the questions and find the answers, but the task gives the students a lot more freedom. We might then say that the task is probably about point B on the graph.

At this point we can ask ourselves an important question: *What is the ultimate aim of language teaching?* Most teachers would probably agree that the ultimate aim is *to develop the student's autonomy in language use.* If we think about the graph, we can see that what we are aiming for is 'freedom' in language use so that the students can use and understand language without the need for any external control or support – that is, towards the bottom left of the graph. Rather than focusing on ways of controlling the language and ideas that students produce, we should always be looking for ways to 'free things up'.

Practical ideas

To end this article, here are five simple ideas that begin to make these changes in classroom work. Each of these ideas involves very small changes but we can see that in each one, the students are making a step from 'consumer' towards 'producer', from 'language specific' work towards 'wider educational goals', and are moving from the top right of the graph towards the bottom left – from control towards freedom.

Practical ideas

1 Do a task, make a task
After doing an exercise, students write a similar exercise for other students. They can exchange exercises or the exercises can be kept in a box so that they can take one if they have time to spare.

2 Do a test, make a test
After doing a simple test, students can write part of a test themselves. With the teacher, they can agree what they have covered during the last few lessons. Different groups can take responsibility for writing different parts of the test. The teacher can collect the parts of the test, correct them, put them together and give them back to the students as *their* test.

3 Stimulate the students' questions first
Before reading or listening to a text, the students can suggest questions that they would like the text to answer – i.e. they can produce their own 'comprehension questions'.

4 Stimulate answers first
If a text comes with comprehension questions, the students can try to answer the questions *before* they read the text. Usually this means that they will have to invent details. They can then read the text to compare ideas.

5 Do a task, share outcomes, make a questionnaire
If the students produce a short text about something (e.g. their favourite animal), they can write a few questions about it (e.g. 'Where does my parrot come from?' or 'What is the name of my cat?'). The teacher can then collect these questions and put them on the board ('Where does Cristina's parrot come from?' etc.). The students' texts can then be stuck on the wall and the students can move around the classroom trying to find the answers to each question.

MIXED ABILITY CLASSROOMS: Turning weakness into strength

Diana Hicks considers the meaning of 'mixed ability' and shows how we can build a greater sense of community in the classroom.

Differing strengths and weaknesses

All classes with more than one student are 'mixed ability' so, in a class of 25 or 30 students, there will be a range of abilities, proficiencies, strengths and weaknesses as there is in any group of 25–30 people. Such heterogeneity in the classroom is often thought of as something to be avoided if possible. The description 'mixed ability' often carries with it negative overtones: many year groups are 'streamed', usually by means of entrance tests, to try to create a feeling of homogeneity so that all the strong (or 'good') students are kept together and the weaker (or 'bad') students work together. The problem is that strengths displayed in an entrance test, which is often a series of grammar-based gap-fill items, may mask weaknesses in other areas. These will gradually reveal themselves over the course of the term or year. Differing strengths and weaknesses, abilities and proficiencies emerge and the class inevitably becomes more and more heterogeneous. This is the 'normal' classroom situation in every school, in every country in the world. So, what are the weaknesses?

Some 'weaknesses' and some suggestions

'Some students don't seem to "catch on" as quickly as the others.'

It is not likely that all 25 students will be able to understand a new structure at the same time because individual students bring to the lesson a range of experience and different areas of knowledge. Perhaps some students have learned this structure elsewhere before, or perhaps others find it hard to hear the explanation, or others find it difficult to be engrossed in the task. The fact that some students, and these may be different ones each time, do not 'catch on' as quickly as some others means that the teaching approach we adopt and the pace we work at have to cater for these differences.

Increasing student confidence and interest

In language learning, increasing the confidence and interest of all the students in the class will automatically lead to real homogeneity. First, confidence can be increased if students know in advance what the next few lessons will be about. Research shows that if we know what we are going to learn, we are more confident and so understand better and more efficiently. Allowing time at the beginning of a lesson for students to look ahead through the next few pages of the coursebook, looking at the pictures, picking out certain kinds of exercises and so on, will make students feel more comfortable about what is going to come. Also, it is often worth setting homework which allows students to preview the next Unit rather than concentrating only on follow-up work for homework. This would be particularly appropriate for lessons which focus on a new structure or have reading passages.

Preview time

'Preview' time also gives students the opportunity to bring more of themselves to the lesson and will enable the lesson to start from the students themselves rather than from an external point of reference which may be difficult for some students to 'hook into'. In this way, all students, irrespective of ability or proficiency, will be able to contribute something to the start of the lesson. Perhaps the starting point for each Unit can be the students asking questions about the topic or text or language area rather than answering questions posed by the book or the teacher. For example, asking the question 'What do you know about the Present continuous/the moon/life in the USA?' will produce, possibly, some answers from a few students and guilt from the others. However, changing the question slightly to 'What DON'T you know about the Present continuous/the moon/life in the USA?' will create a greater feeling of confidence amongst all students and a sense of community enquiry.

Why am I doing this?

If students know why they are doing something, they become more confident. Many students do tasks without fully understanding why they are doing them. Spending a few minutes at the beginning of a Unit asking them to pick out some grammar or vocabulary tasks or tasks which require more accuracy than fluency or vice versa will encourage confidence. The more choice students have over the kinds of task they do to practise new grammar or vocabulary, the more likely they will be to feel confident about their own learning.

Mistakes

All students need to feel comfortable with the fact that they will make mistakes or forget and confuse things. New words, structures and irregular verbs can easily slip through everyone's mind. 'Getting it right' is often an obstacle to 'having a go' and gaining valuable practice. This confident student understood an important feature of learning:

You always get a mark if you try. She's not going to not give you a mark for raising your hand and saying something and saying it wrong. You contributed something and you made a mistake that probably other people have made and you probably helped other people even more.[1]

In other words, students do not need to feel guilty because they have made a mistake.

'Some students work faster than others.'

The second concern with mixed ability classes is the difference in student pace: some students work more quickly than others.

Keeping up the pace

Most lessons work at the teacher's pace: the teacher decides what should be covered in the space of the lesson and how much time should be spent on each task, but, generally, students do not share this information. If students know how long they have to do a task, perhaps by negotiating the time with the teacher, they are more likely to feel confident about tackling the task and will avoid the feeling of guilt associated with not finishing a task on time. Perhaps if the exercise has the traditional ten questions, students may be allowed to decide which six questions they will answer in the time allocated.

Often we find that students are 'slow' at one kind of task but much faster at another. If the students work on a range of different open and closed tasks which use all the skills over a period of, for example, ten lessons, obvious individual variations of pace will emerge. It is always interesting to carry out a case study of three students of different levels and to watch their pace and performance on a wide range of tasks over a specified period. There may be interesting variations in both speed and achievement depending on variables such as the subject matter of the task, the skill required, the way of working (alone, in pairs or groups) and with whom, the position of the task in the sequence or unit (whether it comes at the beginning, middle or end), how much choice the student exercised in doing the task and how positive the teacher felt about how the student would accomplish it.

'I have to provide different tasks for the students to do.'

Variety of task type

Teachers, already overworked, often spend evenings and weekends creating supplementary materials for different levels of student proficiency. However, students who have 'easier' worksheets feel guilty because they are not 'good' enough to do the more difficult ones.

Part of the problem is that many language learning tasks consist of questions which require one correct answer. The students who, for whatever reason, find it more difficult than the others to provide this one correct answer will soon become disillusioned. However, tasks which allow students to provide a range of open answers will appeal to more students more of the time.

For example, after reading a text, instead of answering true/false or comprehension questions, students could be asked to use the text as a basis for creating their own questions. Or students could be asked to 'vandalise' the text in some way: perhaps they could jumble up the sentences in one paragraph or the words in some of the sentences, or perhaps they could add words, such as adverbs or adjectives to individual sentences and ask their partners to find the changes they have made. Perhaps they could add whole sentences to a paragraph. The purpose of this type of task is to involve all the students in tasks which not only require them to use language they already know, and to do something which is different from the other students, but also to make decisions about how they will do a task. They do not feel guilty that they have not done the same as the other students because that is not the aim of the exercise.

'The slower ones begin to feel more and more inadequate.'

Who is slow at what?

Many students feel that they are 'bad' at English. However, it is unlikely that they will be 'bad' at every aspect of language learning. The term 'mixed ability' more safely refers to the mixture of abilities which we all have. We may be very good at cooking main courses, for example, but not so good at making cakes or vice versa. We cannot accurately describe ourselves as 'bad at cooking' if that is the case. We are more likely to say 'I'm hopeless at making cakes but my lasagne always tastes good'.

Within one domain, we all have strengths and weaknesses: even within the domain of our own second language use, there will be areas of strength and weakness. If students learn more precisely where their strengths and weaknesses are in English they will be more likely to judge themselves like this:

My spelling is pretty good, but my pronunciation needs practice.

I'm very good at the listening exercises, but I'm not so good at reading.

Conclusion

Once they are aware of their individual weaknesses, students will understand that all the other students have weaknesses too and will be less likely to dismiss themselves as guilty of being 'bad at English'. Every student is 'mixed ability' and every class is 'mixed ability'. Lockstep teaching, where each student has to move ahead at the same time as the others, draws attention to the negative aspects of heterogeneity. Allowing room for the students to display their strengths in different skills draws attention to the positive aspects of individual variations.

[1] Brandes, D and Ginnis, P (1986): *A Guide to Student-Centred Learning*, published by Blackwell.

CLASSROOM RESEARCH

Andrew Littlejohn explains how any teacher can do their own classroom research as a part of their normal teaching.

As teachers, we are puzzled by what happens – or doesn't happen – in the classroom. Why don't the students speak English when they are working in groups? Why do they have difficulty with spelling? Why don't they listen to the instructions? Why do they make the same mistakes again and again? Why do they misbehave so much? and so on. In the normal course of teaching it is usually difficult to find time to reflect on *why* these things happen. The result is that we often begin to accept things as they are ('Class 2 is very weak') or we look for simple, handy explanations ('They're lazy', 'They're tired').

In actual fact, however, teaching and learning is a very complex process. We still know very little about *how* people learn a language – that is, exactly what happens inside the brain. Added to that fact, a classroom is itself a very complex setting. If we bring ten, twenty, thirty or more people together in the same room and ask them to work together, it is not surprising that things do not work exactly the way one person – the teacher – expects it to work. Each student, an individual, will bring with them their own ideas, experiences, interests and physical and emotional states. The complex nature of teaching and learning make it even more important, then, that we try to understand *why* things happen the way they do in the classroom – and how it might be possible to change things if necessary.

Teacher's questions

Teachers often have many questions. Here are some very common examples, which most teachers have asked themselves at one time or another:

- How can I make my students speak ENGLISH?
- How can I cope with their mixed abilities and varied interests?
- How can I motivate my students and sustain that motivation?
- How can I make them behave?!

Each question is almost a plea for help, for teaching is often difficult. Behind each question we can imagine the situation that might have prompted the teacher to ask the question. For example, the first question often comes from a situation in which students drop into their mother tongue once they are put into groups. In an attempt to solve the situation, the teacher might invent ingenious ways to encourage the students to speak English – giving rewards to students that speak English the most, or fining students who use the mother tongue. More often than not, however, these solutions only bring a temporary change – and after a short time the teacher is back once again trying to find another strategy to use. The reason why these 'quick solutions' do not usually work is that they are often based on a simple explanation (e.g. 'They're lazy', 'They're shy') of what we have seen is an incredibly complex matter. This means that if we want to find more permanent solutions we have to look more deeply into things. In other words, we have to do some *research*.

The term 'research' often sounds very distant and academic. We perhaps have images of 'experts' in laboratories with elaborate equipment. In actual fact, *any* teacher can do research as part of his or her normal teaching – and the benefits of doing it are enormous. Teachers are the 'experts' of their classrooms – they will know more about their students than any outsider will know. If teachers do their own research it can help them understand *their* classrooms and improve *their* teaching and *their* students' learning. 'Research' need not be complicated or difficult. We can think of two basic approaches: '*research by thinking*' and '*research by experimenting*'. The second type will always involve the first type, but we can often learn a lot about what happens in the classroom simply by thinking more deeply about it.

Research by thinking

The best way to explain 'research by thinking' is to take an example. Let's take the example I gave earlier:

How can I make my students speak ENGLISH?

The usual response to the question is immediately to start trying to find the answer – the 'quick solutions' I mentioned earlier. However, if we want to understand the situation that is causing the problem, the first thing that we have to do is to *think* about it. We can ask ourselves some more questions. Look at each word in the question. What does the question tell you about the situation? For example, the word 'I' might suggest that the teacher is taking all the decisions. Maybe that simple fact is causing the problem. Maybe the students do not feel that they are part of the lesson. Similarly, the word 'make' might suggest that the teacher is looking for ways to *force* the students – and the students may be reacting to being pushed into doing something. Here are some more ideas that might come from analysing the question.

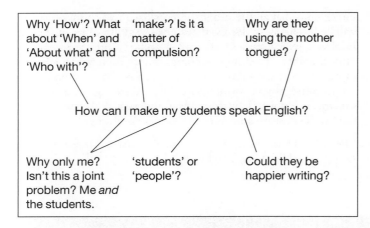

Why 'How'? What about 'When' and 'About what' and 'Who with'?

'make'? Is it a matter of compulsion?

Why are they using the mother tongue?

How can I make my students speak English?

Why only me? Isn't this a joint problem? Me *and* the students.

'students' or 'people'?

Could they be happier writing?

- Maybe they are not happy with the people they are working with.
- Maybe they feel shy.
- Maybe they don't feel involved in the lesson.

The list can go on and on but the teacher can select what seems to be the most likely causes and then experiment – make some changes in the classroom and see if the situation improves. If only one change is made at a time it will be easier to see if there is any effect. Here are some examples.

Possible cause	Things to experiment with
Maybe they don't like the topics.	Ask them to suggest or choose the topics.
Maybe they are tired when we do groupwork.	Try groupwork before the break or earlier in the week.
Maybe they are not happy with the people they are working with.	Try changing pairs/groups – or let them choose who they work with.
Maybe they feel shy.	Avoid 'public' groupwork. Let them record their conversations.
Maybe they don't feel involved in the lesson.	Try sharing the planning of the lesson with them, how long you will spend on activities, who they will work with, etc.

Monitoring what happens after each experiment can reveal a lot. Of course, every lesson is unique, so what is successful one day may not necessarily be successful another day, but the process of experimenting and observing what happens can help the teacher understand more deeply what happens in the classroom and so lead to more effective teaching and learning.

If we look carefully at the question in this way, we can often begin to see the probable cause of the problem and so begin to make changes in the classroom. For example, if a teacher decided that the students might not feel that they are part of what happens in the classroom, he or she might begin trying to involve the students in planning the groupwork in some way. This 'research by thinking' can have a great impact.

Sometimes, however, our thinking might identify a number of possible explanations and possible solutions so it may be difficult to decide what to do next. This takes us to the next approach to research: *research by experimenting*.

Research by experimenting

Taking the example that we looked at just now, we can see that there might be a lot of different reasons why the students don't speak English in groups. Here is a list of just some possible explanations.

- Maybe they don't like the topics.
- Maybe they are tired when we do groupwork.

EVALUATION AND ASSESSMENT: Can they go hand in hand?

Diana Hicks looks at some differences between assessment and evaluation and suggests some practical classroom strategies.

New approaches and ideas in the curriculum, teacher training, classroom activities and teaching styles bring with them new ways of thinking and behaving and new words to talk about the innovations. 'Evaluation' and 'assessment' are two examples of this new vocabulary. Neither term is new to teachers or students but what is new are the different strategies which can be used to make clearer distinctions between them.

Evaluation and assessment are often thought of as having the same meaning because they can sometimes be carried out by one event. However, each serves different purposes because assessment and evaluation are each concerned with different aspects of teaching and learning. We assess our students to establish *what* and *how much* they have learned but we evaluate our students to find out *how* the learning process is developing. Both are of importance to the teacher and the learners.

Assessment without evaluation

The most straightforward example of assessment without evaluation is the end of year examinations. These are usually based on the syllabus or the textbook and the grade indicates the 'attainment' or 'achievement' level of each student, which can be measured against the other students in the same class or in other classes. The result is simply that students know whether they have passed or failed and teachers know who are the 'good', 'average' and 'weak' students.

Assessment with evaluation

However, in addition to end of year tests, during the course of a school year students may take other smaller 'quizzes' or tests. Generally, however, the scores from these smaller tests (such as 6/10 or 62%) will give the teacher the rank order for the students in the class but will probably not tell the students where and why they are going wrong, nor will it give them strategies to help them improve. Neither will the scores inform the teacher about how and why the students behaved in a certain way. These smaller tests are ideal mechanisms to use to 'observe effects in context' – in other words, to build evaluation into assessment.

Some practical ideas

Tests in the school year

Tests given during the school year can be seen as ways to help bring about changes in our teaching. In this way they move away from being merely 'attainment' or 'achievement' tests and instead become 'formative' or 'diagnostic'. In this case evaluation is used to improve certain aspects of the course or to change or add different activities in order to improve the progress of more of the students in the class during the course of the school year.

The short tests given during the year usually refer back to units recently covered in class and usually focus on grammar and vocabulary. Often they are 'gap fill' so the teacher or even students can mark them quickly. These provide quantitative feedback – they tell us how much the students have remembered – but they do not tell us how they learned it or which kind of tasks the students found most useful to help them understand it. However, if the students are involved in evaluating the contents of the test, we can acquire qualitative feedback on the basis of which we can reassess our teaching and testing behaviours. There are different ways in which students can be involved in this qualitative process of assessment and evaluation.

Evaluation in vocabulary assessment: involving the students

First, all tests consist of 'what' and 'how': students usually know 'what' they will be tested on but they are probably not told 'how'. We often underestimate the 'how': that is, the exercise type we choose may not be a factor taken into account when we design the test. Nevertheless, it is this 'how' of the test which can help us make our teaching and the students' learning more effective. We can bring the students into the process of 'how' by, for example, telling them that there will be a vocabulary test and inviting them to think about what kind of exercise would test their knowledge of vocabulary best. First, students can look at the kinds of vocabulary exercises they did in previous tests. If the vocabulary exercise in all the tests is always the same type it will be worth spending some time thinking about why this is the case.

Exercise types

If, however, there is a range of exercise types which test vocabulary, students can be asked to consider how successful they think each exercise type is: how much guesswork is involved in each exercise? what kind of guesswork? Guessing from context in a cloze text, for example, is a different kind of guessing from three or four choices in a multiple choice sentence. What other language knowledge do they use to make guesses in multiple choice sentences? Which kinds of exercise ask them to think about the words? Which ones ask them to use the words creatively? Which exercise types require other skills? (Comprehension questions require reading skills for example.) Which kind of exercise do they prefer and why?

Then, to get a broader picture, students can look through their Student's Books and Workbooks and find as many different kinds of vocabulary exercises as they can, and, at the same time, they can consider which types are appropriate to use in a test. By this time, a list of different vocabulary exercise test types can be written on the board and students can be asked to rank them in order on a piece of paper: putting the ones which they like and are good at at the top and the ones they don't like and are not so good at at the bottom. In pairs they can then discuss reasons for their reactions and write them on their sheet. The sheets are collected in and the results are collated on a poster or overhead transparency.

Already the students have been able to evaluate 'how' they are tested, to think about a variety of options and to think about which type of exercise suits them best. The teacher has collected in some important qualitative information about the process of testing which can be used to inform the construction of the next test and, perhaps also, the teaching which leads up to the next test.

The next test

The next test can be prepared in the normal way except that, on the test paper, the teacher can put two or possibly three different kinds of exercises to test the same material from which the students have a choice: they must do the exercise which they think they will do best at. The teacher marks the test as usual but at the same time, makes a note of the choices the students made and checks whether students did better or worse than they did on previous tests. When the test is returned to the students they will know not just how much they know but also how correct they were in their choice. In other words, they will have learned something more about their own learning strength.

This kind of evaluation process allows the teacher to understand more about the individual students' learning preferences but also shows that often it may not be the material, in this case, the vocabulary, which is causing a problem for the students, but the manner – the way – in which it is being tested, or, possibly even being taught. This kind of approach to a test allows for the results to become the next stage of the teaching process and the next stage of the students' learning process.

Students' follow up: vocabulary learning

Tests are often graded by the teacher, returned to the students, the correct answers are provided in class and the test is then put away and forgotten. If the students have chosen which part of the test to do, the success or failure of that choice can become a subject of discussion: how did they prepare for the vocabulary test? What different approaches did they use and why? Finding out what students do to help themselves learn provides fundamental qualitative data for all teachers. Some students may not prepare well for a test because they are not sure what to do or they know that the strategies they have used before have been unsuccessful and they don't know how to replace them. Unless they learn other strategies they may stop preparing for tests altogether because they know they will fail. Some students may like to keep an evaluation 'diary' or journal in which they can record what kinds of strategies they used to prepare for tests or learn their new vocabulary.

Students spend about 10,000 hours of their lifetime trying to learn at school: it is important that some of those hours are spent on evaluating and discussing how that learning happens, or doesn't happen!

Teachers' follow up: vocabulary teaching

Once the students have discussed their successes, failures and strategies, the teacher can then decide how to adapt vocabulary teaching in the future. Perhaps too much time is spent on 'pre-teaching' vocabulary? Perhaps students know more words than the teacher thinks? Perhaps they know different ones? Perhaps students do not feel comfortable with dictionaries? Perhaps the problem isn't one of vocabulary but of spelling? Perhaps there is too much emphasis on short-term memory rather than long-term memory? Perhaps some students would prefer more vocabulary practice in a variety of ways – more reading, more puzzles, more writing?

Assessment in writing

Many students find writing in English very difficult because there are so many different things to get right – spelling, tenses, vocabulary, agreements, prepositions, syntax: particularly word order, register, punctuation and organisation. Correcting written work is often very time consuming and frequently ineffective in that it changes little in the students' approach in the future. When students produce a piece of writing it can be marked subjectively or holistically. This means that an overall grade is given which does not take into account specific strengths and weaknesses such as spelling, sentence structure or punctuation but is concerned with the general impression. This is an assessment strategy which has no built-in evaluation. Students do not know from a holistic mark where their weak points are or what they should do to improve. On the other hand, correcting every error in the writing has little or no evaluative worth either because it often leaves students feeling that they don't know where to start to improve.

Evaluation in writing

In order to build evaluation into the assessment of writing during the course it is worth having an analytic marking scheme which the students are familiar with. If, for example, the piece of writing has a total of 20 marks, separate marks need to be allocated for each aspect of the writing. The teacher can put on the blackboard a list of the features to correct in a piece of writing and ask the students to decide how many marks they think should be given to each feature (with the total amounting to 20). When the students have a writing test or produce a piece of writing in class or for homework, marks can be given for each individual feature, e.g. 2/4 spelling, 3/5 punctuation, etc. Before the students hand in the work, they can be asked to write their own grades for each feature at the bottom of the paper. This will encourage students not only to look through their work carefully when they have finished but will also help them evaluate their own weak and strong points.

Follow up: writing

A breakdown of areas for marking will give the students a clearer idea of their strengths and weaknesses. Students who have spelling problems, for example, can be asked to analyse what kind of mistakes they make, perhaps to compare them with patterns of spelling errors in mother tongue. The teacher may then need to provide spelling worksheets or the students can be asked to prepare spelling quizzes. If all the students are weak on cohesion – that is, if the texts they write do not hang together well – it may be worth spending time analysing the texts in the Student's Book or in other resources. Perhaps on one test, the students can be allowed to have English-English dictionaries, on the next test they could be allowed to take in English-mother tongue dictionaries. The teacher can then discuss with them afterwards the differences this made to their writing. Perhaps some students write and think very slowly and this affects their work. In this case the next writing test can be set with double the time limit, making sure there is something else for the students who finish early to do.

Assessment and evaluation cannot always walk hand in hand: assessment is needed for administration purposes, teachers, parents, students, employers and universities. However, the process of teaching and learning can benefit enormously from the flexibility provided by building evaluative systems into smaller assessment tests so that ongoing testing becomes a 'user-friendly' 'hand holding' activity rather than an isolating threat.